You are God's Gift to the World

The Purpose of Your Life on Earth

Louis M. Savary with Patricia H. Berne

BALBOA.
PRESS
A DIVISION OF HAY HOUSE

Balboa Press books may be ordered through booksellers or by contacting:

Balboa Press
A Division of Hay House
1663 Liberty Drive
Bloomington, IN 47403
www.balboapress.com
1-(877) 407-4847

Printed in the United States of America

ISBN: 978-1-4525-6644-3 (sc)
ISBN: 978-1-4525-6645-0 (e)

Library of Congress Control Number: 2013900007

Balboa Press rev. date: 1/7/2012

Table of Contents

DEDICATION

To Rev. Tom Composto (1936-2011), dearest friend of fifty years, whose life dedicated to transforming the world, person by person in the ghettos of Baltimore, inspired this book.

Introduction

Who Are You?

"Who do you think you are, God's gift to the world?"

As four-year-old Mary's mother was seated in a living room chair reading, Mary, feeling joyous and full of energy, came into the living room and proudly began to jump around and dance in front of her mother as if she were a ballerina. When her dance came to an end, she grinned at her mother, expecting some acknowledgement.

Instead, her mother looked up from her book and insultingly said, "Who do you think you are, God's gift to the world?"

At a workshop, after hearing Mary's story, a grown man told us a similar story.

"In high school," he said, "I thoughtlessly spoke those same words to a fellow student who had told me about something he had accomplished that he was proud of. I don't recall what it was that he had achieved, I only remember that I was jealous of him and wanted to make fun of him. I said, *Who do you think you are, God's gift to the world?* I know my comment hurt him."

I suspect many of our readers have heard that same putdown or some taunting comment like it, addressed to them and been emotionally wounded by it. Perhaps some have even used that expression, as the young man did, as a barb to taunt, tease or insult another person who had achieved some desired goal.

"Today," the man at the workshop explained, "I wish I had the chance to retract what I said many years ago to my fellow student. I wish I had the chance to say to him what I now realize is true. 'You were and are God's gift to the world. Your accomplishment that I belittled back then was truly doing God's work in the world.'"

This book was written to transform this false and hurtful comment once and for all and, instead, apply it as a positive affirmation to everyone. It shouts to all, *"You are important. You are needed. You are God's gift to the world!"*

Even more, it shows how being God's gift to the world is your highest calling in life.

This wonderful affirmation—You are God's gift to the world—is true of each one of us. God gave you and me to the world to help make it a better place. It has been God's plan all along to continually renew the face of the Earth. To have a role in this divine enterprise of transforming the world is your highest human purpose.

God has placed this grand Earth renewal project into our human hands. We have been entrusted with a wondrous dignity. In this time and place, we are involved in it individually and collectively. We all share the same general purpose. But we each do it uniquely, in our own way. Each of us is called to help humanity move forward in love by caring for each other and for our Earth. It is what we affirm when we cry out in prayer:

Thy kingdom come!
Thy will be done on Earth

It is so simple. *Thy will be done on Earth.* We want God's divine plan to be accomplished on Earth. We want God's spirit of love and caring—God's reign—to cover the Earth. And there are billions of us who truly care. And for this reason, you and I along with those other billions are called to carry out God's plan to renew the face of our world. In accepting that you are God's gift to the world, you connect yourself with something far larger than yourself. You become part of God's very own project for our world.

This is the reason God created you at this moment in history. This is the reason God created all the others you will encounter during your lifetime, so that you and all the others can help that forward movement in billions of ways, great and small, toward God's vision for us. This is your supreme purpose for being born in the particular family, town and country where you were born. This is why, no matter what anyone says, you are important. To God, you are unique and irreplaceable.

Deep inside, you know that you have been called to make a positive difference in the world. It is written in your mind and heart. That longing is written genetically in everyone. You can feel the truth of it engraved in your soul because God wrote it there! As you come to accept yourself as gift to the world, you learn to imbue each person or thing you touch with sacredness. And your whole life becomes a prayer and a blessing.

What is deepest in us is of God. Just as God created beauty everywhere, we are rooted in that divine beauty. Just as God made everything out of love, we too have emerged from within the warmth of that divine Love. Just as God made the light in the beginning, we are called to be bearers of that light into the future.

No two people have exactly the same calling. Neither your brother nor your sister has the same role in God's plan as you. Neither do your parents. Neither do your children. No one else has exactly the same opportunities you do to make a positive difference. No one can substitute for you. That is why you are unique. That is why you are irreplaceable. That is why you are God's gift to the world.

It is up to you to do what you have been put on Earth to do—to do your part in helping transform the face of the Earth. To do it is your calling. To do it is your privilege. To do it is your destiny. This task is not reserved for prophets or mystics, scientists or artists. It belongs to all people. It can only be a global and universal effort. It will require many decisions of billions of individual persons responding to the urgings of the divine spirit.

It is important to point out here that many people—probably most people—may never know that they are God's gift to the world. Most seldom think about the fact that they are living out their God-given purpose. Perhaps no one has ever told them. No matter. They still contribute their gifts and abilities to God's work. Unaware, but following their heart, they can still be doing their part to renew the face of the Earth. They make their unique and important contribution unwittingly, simply by faithfully fulfilling their roles in life.

Such people do things, even create major positive changes in their communities, not because they think they are going to be seen as important or get recognized. They do it because they believe it needs to be done. Because the impulse to do it springs from a place deep within their souls.

During the time of slavery in the United States, Harriet Tubman was a freed woman slave, who had no need ever to return to the South where she would certainly be enslaved again if she were caught. Yet she returned again and again to free hundreds of other slaves using what was called the Underground Railroad to the North.

In 2010, the 65-year-old Aung San Suu Kyi of Burma was awarded the Nobel Peace Prize for her nonviolent resistance on behalf of the millions of Burmese people oppressed and impoverished by a military junta who controlled Burma for over fifty years. She dared to continue to stand up to the military generals of the regime, even though they had kept her locked up in prison for 15 of the past 21 years. Why did she not just remain a quiet woman? "My very top priority," she said, "is for people to understand that they have the power to change things themselves." And she set the example for them.[1]

Marc Gold has been called a shoestring philanthropist.[2] He gives people small donations of money so they can get started making it on their own. In India, he met a Tibetan refugee who needed a hearing aid so she could return to work and her son could go to school. He bought her a hearing aid for $35. "I thought you had to be wealthy to make a difference," he said. With another small donation from him, a widow was able to buy a sewing machine and start a business. In China, he paid a mechanic $40 to fix a taxi driver's rickshaw so the driver could keep earning a living. To a Tibetan orphanage school he gave ten soccer balls. Marc Gold now has *100 Friends* who give him small amounts of money from time to time. And he returns to Asia transforming people's lives a few dollars at a time.

These are just three examples of people who saw a need, and they happened to be there to respond. They felt an inner call to say "yes" to that need. It's an attitude that all of us can emulate. "It changes you inside," said one of Marc's friends, "when you have a chance to do these things."

I'm sure at times, when facing the size of the tasks before them, each of these people felt that it might be too much for them to accomplish, or even undertake, yet they went ahead and did it—or at least they tried.

May we all be that courageous.

"I don't know what your destiny will be," wrote Albert Schweitzer, "but one thing I know: The only ones among you who will be really happy are those who have sought and found how to serve."

For Dr. Mehmet Oz, the famous physician television personality, finding and having a purpose in life that is of service to others is one

---

1   Hannah Beech, "The First Lady of Freedom," *Time Magazine*, Jan. 10, 2011, p. 32.

2   Linda Arking, "The Shoestring Philanthropist," *Parade Magazine*, Dec. 19, 2010, p. 8.

big secret to enjoying good health. "I've performed open-heart surgeries for 17 years and I repeatedly hear the same post-op request from a patient's worried spouse: 'Please tell my hard-charging significant other to retire.' And not once have I done it, no matter how reasonable the request. That's because I believe, deeply, that having purpose in your life is the key to good health."[3] And having a purpose doesn't stop with retirement. As long as you are still breathing, you have a purpose.

Having a purpose for living is good not only for your personal physical and mental health but also for the health of our planet and for the success of God's work in the world.

Notice that, though for some people their job or occupation may be part of their purpose or destiny, your life purpose is always much larger and broader than any job. Dr. Oz's recommendation was not that heart attack survivors should keep working for the same company till the day they die, but that no matter where people were in life they need to find a purpose, someplace where their contribution can make a positive difference. Freeing slaves wasn't Harriet Tubman's occupation (she was a house servant and a field worker), nor was fighting for Burma's freedom the occupation of Aung San Suu Kyi (she was a writer of biographies and juvenile books), nor was giving mini gifts to foreigners the occupation of Marc Gold (he was a special education teacher of children with severe learning disabilities).

If you are unclear about what you have been called by God to do with your life or how you were meant to make a difference in the world, some suggestions in these pages may help in making that discovery. You will also find some ideas about how to carry it out, perhaps better and more effectively than you otherwise might. Included are many fascinating and surprising stories of people living out a purpose they have discovered. Let these stories remind you that you, too, can make a difference.

So, why not say "yes"?

In the wise words of twelve-year-old Anne Frank, "How wonderful it is that nobody need wait a single moment before starting to improve the world!"

---

3   Dr. Mehmet Oz, M.D., "Feel Your Best." *AARP The Magazine*, May/June 2011, p. 20.

Part I

RECOGNIZING

You Are God's Gift to the World

Chapter 1

Things Big and Small

Bigger Things

As you become aware of being God's gift to the world—and accept responsibility for living it out—you will realize you have work to do in two broad categories. You will feel called to do some *bigger things* plus a lot of *smaller things.*

Sometimes the most important "ability" you can develop as God's gift to the world is response-ability. This is the ability to sense what you are being called to do each day and to do it, as best you can.

You cannot change a moment of the past, but you can live to your best each moment of today.

"I expect to pass through life but once," said William Penn, the Quaker exile from England who founded Pennsylvania in 1681. "If therefore, there be any kindness I can show or any good thing I can do to any fellow being, let me do it now, and not defer or neglect it, as I shall not pass this way again."

Penn's remarks reflect a kind of inner awareness intended for all persons by God, right from the beginnings of human life. It is an awareness that recognizes God's involvement in everything happening on Earth. This awareness reveals to us that somehow *the world itself is permeated by the divine spirit.*

With this awareness, we learn to "see" not only the inner meaning of things, but we also learn to use this inner sense to manage our lives and our time, and how we use and care for all the rest of things on Earth.

Even Bigger Things

As examples of bigger things, consider some of the great explorers, statesmen, inventors, artists, scientists, authors, politicians that brought about great positive differences that affected the whole world.[4]

The Wright brothers, Orville and Wilbur, taught us that humans could fly. They crashed and failed many, many times before they succeeded in keeping a plane airborne. In this, they taught us never to give up. Today, we fly to the moon and Mars, and think little of it.

In the midst of the Great Depression, two poor youngsters, Joe Shuster and Jerry Siegel, who used to draw their cartoons on the back of butcher's paper, gave us the world's first great hero, *Superman*. Even though comic book publishers at first rejected the idea of a superhero, these cartoonists finally succeeded. They instilled hope in an otherwise depressed young generation and gave us the idea that ordinary people could be heroes.

For forty years, Fred Rogers was the television host of *Mr. Roger's Neighborhood*. On his show, he taught kindness to generations of children. Day after day for decades, in thousands of little and big ways, Mr. Rogers showed us how to be gentle, compassionate, thoughtful and to love nature.

Amelia Earhart, the first female to fly across the Atlantic, was a high-flying daredevil. She lost her life attempting to be the first female to circumnavigate the globe by airplane. "Women must try to do things as men have tried," she said. "When they fail, their failure must be but a challenge to others." She also wisely said, "Never interrupt someone doing something that *you* said couldn't be done."

Many of the songs written by John Lennon of *Beatles* fame were anthems advocating peace during the war in Vietnam, even when the FBI was tapping his phones. With courage and his guitar, he redefined what a rock star *can* shout about.

Albert Einstein created the theory of relativity and won the Nobel Prize in physics. This man, who was the greatest scientist of the 20th century, didn't learn to speak until he was three years old. His schoolteachers called him a foolish dreamer. He proved them all wrong. In his maturity he became an advocate for peace and spirituality. He

---

4   For many of the following examples, I am indebted to novelist Brad Meltzer who created the wonderfully inspiring book *Heroes for My Son*. New York: HarperCollins, 2010.

wrote, "One cannot help being in awe when one contemplates the mysteries of eternity, of life, of the marvelous structures of reality."

We think of Mark Twain, author of *The Adventures of Huckleberry Finn*, primarily as a humorist and fiction writer. But, while Huckleberry Finn appears to us today to be just a story about a boy on the Mississippi River, in its pages when it was first published the book waged a most powerful fight against injustice and slavery. Mark Twain showed the power of a story that told the truth. "Always do right," he said. "This will gratify some people and astonish the rest."

These are just some of the people who taught us about love, compassion, dedication, determination, courage and the power of human creativity. There are thousands of stories like these. Look around you, everywhere, and you'll find proof. You'll find examples of these qualities—like charity, truthfulness, leadership with humility, modesty and dignity.

Wealthy People

Wealthy people have many opportunities to do significant things on a large scale.

Everyone has heard of the Bill and Melinda Gates Foundation, dedicated to bringing innovations in health, development and learning to the global community. Bill Gates is one of the richest humans in the world, having made his fortune creating Microsoft software for computers. With software, he has already transformed much of the Earth in its ability to communicate. Now, Bill and his wife have dedicated themselves to making a positive difference through philanthropy. Today, they fund medical research such as vaccines for diseases like HIV/AIDS, polio and meningitis, diseases that decimate people in Africa, India and elsewhere. They fund innovative educational projects for improvement of teachers and the art of teaching. They support many programs of technological research in the United States as well as in Third World countries, such as better irrigation methods and higher crop yields.

Another philanthropic billionaire that mostly only Californians know is Eli Broad (rhymes with code), who made his billions in tract housing and insurance. As a singular patron of the arts, he has been called the Lorenzo de' Medici of Los Angeles. Since his retirement in

1999, he has given away more than two billion dollars. "A map of the city dotted with contributions bearing his name looks almost pointillist: thirty-six million dollars to biological research at the California Institute of Technology, fifty million to the Broad Contemporary Art Museum, a hundred million to charter schools, thirty million to stem-cell research at the University of Southern California, ten million to the Broad Stage, a new performing-arts center, seven million to the Los Angeles Opera."[5] Some billionaires are doing their share of renewing the face of the Earth.

Little Things that Turn Out to be Big Things

Even though you and I may not be famous billionaires—or millionaires or even "comfortably well off"—each of us is called to do some things that are big and important. It is likely that the "big things" that most of us do will probably not make the Evening News on television. But in God's eyes, they are still important.

For example, you might talk a teenager out of committing suicide, a transformational encounter no one knows about except you and the teen. And that young person may grow up to be a major league sports star or a physician or a diplomat—someone God needed to be precisely in a certain position at a certain time.

Or you may be influential in helping a young mother give up an addiction to alcohol or drugs, and she goes on to become a great parent and may even become a speaker in schools about the importance of not abusing alcohol or drugs.

The big things we will be called upon to do will usually involve some kind of work or service—something we are good at—that will make a great positive difference in the present and future lives of individuals, families or groups. Sometimes it might just be the coincidence of being in the right place at the right time.

"Each of us can work to change a small portion of events," said Robert F. Kennedy, who was assassinated while running for the presidency of the United States, "and in the total of all those deeds will be written the history of this generation."

<hr />

5   Connie Bruck, "The Art of the Billionaire," *The New Yorker*. December 6, 2010, p. 50.

Extra Things

Yet many of us will feel called upon from time to time to go beyond doing our jobs, and to do some other special things.

Nelson Mandella felt committed to change South Africa's social and political policy of racial repression. He was sent to prison for 27 years because he was a political activist. When he got out, he somehow managed to fulfill his calling—he negotiated the end of legal racial segregation in his country—and to become South Africa's president in its first truly free election.

Neil Armstrong was the first human to set foot on the moon, but it took him a thousand steps and fearless determination to get there. He felt the inner desire to fly at an early age. He got his pilot's license at 16. By the time he was 30, he had tested over two hundred different aircraft, including the X-15 rocket plane.

Jackie Robinson, a black man, accepted the challenge to change American professional baseball—and all sports—when he crossed the color barrier for the first time and literally risked his life to play for the Brooklyn Dodgers in the late 1940s. Despite jeers from other ball players and fans in the stands during that first season, despite hate letters and death threats in the mail and by phone, he practiced self-control on and off the playing field.

Lucille Ball felt in her heart that it was a good thing to make people laugh and feel happy, even though her grandmother who raised her told her that happiness was a sin. Lucy never believed her grandmother. In her television series *I love Lucy* she became one of the greatest comedians of all time. With her show she proved to the world that humor was a way to learn to love yourself. "Love yourself first," she said, "and everything falls into line."

Lucy is not advocating being self-centered or egotistical, just realizing how individuals can be a gift to the world, each one in his or her own way.

Dr. Jonas Salk saw the devastation the disease polio was causing, and felt impelled to find a vaccine. After testing drug after drug for eight years, working sixteen-hour days seven days a week, in 1955 he finally found a vaccine against polio. With his discovery he stopped a worldwide epidemic. When a journalist asked him who held the legal patent on this vaccine, Dr. Salk simply replied, "Well, the people, I would say. There is no patent. Could you patent the sun?"

When as a relief worker Dan West saw hungry persons, he felt the urge in his heart to help them in a way different from handing out food. He had a simple idea. He thought: Why not give them a cow rather than a bowl of food? So, Dan West began sending livestock overseas to poverty-stricken places. That was the beginning of Heifer International. The only rule he set for those receiving a gift animal was that when your animal mated and gave birth, you gave the newborn to another family.

You are not Nelson Mandella, Neil Armstrong, Jackie Robinson, Lucille Ball, Jonas Salk or Dan West. You are you. You are a unique single life. Is there something special you are called to?

"Every single life becomes great," said the well-known motivational speaker Brian Tracy, "when the individual sets upon a goal or goals which they really believe in, which they can really commit themselves to, which they can put their whole heart and soul into."

If nothing else, just do something positive every day, no matter how small or insignificant it may seem to you. It will not be wasted.

Failure and Success

Abraham Lincoln is universally recognized as one of the greatest American presidents, but he had numerous failures in his career. In the long run, he was a very successful politician and lawyer. However, his setbacks show that even a "failure" can become president, if he or she doesn't give up.

Among some of his setbacks and disappointments, Lincoln lost his job at the age of 22. In the following year he was defeated in running for the Illinois State Legislature. Note that he was only 23-years old at the time. At age 25, he started a store in New Salem, Illinois, with a partner, but the business failed within a year when the partner died. The next year, Lincoln's sweetheart, Ann Rutledge, died. The following year, at age 27, Lincoln reportedly had a nervous breakdown. At age 29, he was defeated in running for Illinois House Speaker. A few years later he was defeated in a run for nomination for U.S. Congress. Three years later, in 1846, he was elected to Congress, but lost re-nomination two years later. The following year, he was rejected when he sought a land officer position. In 1854, he was defeated in a run for the U.S. Senate. Two years later, he sought nomination for Vice President of his party, but was not chosen. In 1858, he was again defeated in a run for the U.S. Senate. By 1859, even with all these setbacks, Lincoln had created a very successful and lucrative law practice, so only hesitantly did he agree to run for the presidency. In 1860, at the age of 51, Lincoln became President of the United States. You wonder how he ever made it to the top. But when you really think of it, to run for office or high positions so many times, despite failures, you have to have some inner drive to ultimately succeed.

In the end, what we truly admire about Lincoln is that he was true to himself. "I am not bound to win," he said of himself when he was running for president, "but I am bound to be true. I am not bound to succeed, but I am bound to live by the light that I have."

If you are trying to accomplish important things, you will inevitably face a number of setbacks. It is important not to forget or overlook the setbacks or defeats, for we all must face them and learn from them. Abraham Lincoln is a model of perseverance. He shows us that people with determination can overcome life's difficulties.

"Keep away from people who try to belittle your ambitions," said Mark Twain. "Small people always do that, but the really great make you feel that you, too, can become great."

Although you may be one of those called to do something really great to renew the face of the Earth, much of Earth's renewal work will be done in much smaller ways, ways that knit us together as a human family through very basic acts of love and caring.

Chapter 2
Small Positive Differences

When one turns on the television news or picks up a newspaper or a magazine, it can be very easy to give up on our world. There seems to be so much wrong and broken all around us. Even among the various religious leaders and institutions we find much that is wounded, wrong and broken.

We need not use these inexcusable incidents as an excuse to hide our faith or to run away from it. Many in the world criticize and ridicule those who have faith in God and what God is doing in our world. Some even try to convince us that God doesn't exist. But the wrong and brokenness all around us only indicate how much God needs all of us for the necessary healing and growth to take place. Each of us, believers and nonbelievers alike, must make our own truly authentic response to these needs.

The fact is that God is such an unfathomable mystery that even believers, who label God with their various theological concepts, exalted names, eternal qualities and vibrant statements of faith, cannot even begin to scratch the surface of who God is. What we do know for certain is that the founders of every known religion have preached compassion for all people and respect for the well being of every creature on the planet. Every religion is grounded in service to one another and concern for all life.

Cooperating with God

Instead of spending effort in trying to conceptualize God, focus on what God may be asking you to do. Focus on cooperating with God and what God is trying to do among us. Renew your commitment to be involved in the world and its spiritual transformation. Pray always and never lose heart. God needs your help to renew the face of the Earth. You are God's gift to the world—especially to that part of the world where you can make a positive difference, a difference that only you can make.

It is amazing how many people do not realize the positive (and sometimes negative) impact they have on others, even life-changing impacts, just by a few words or a simple action. Sometimes, when we are generous and compassionate in small, barely detectable ways, it can change someone's life forever.

Whether you live in a majestic mansion or a crowded tenement, your smile this morning may help turn another's attitude from negative to positive. Your hug this afternoon may give someone the courage to carry on with hope. Your outstretched, welcoming arms this evening may keep a person from self-harm.

Each person has many opportunities every day to make small positive differences. Each of us has as many chances as anyone else to do the little things that help renew the Earth, no matter what our state in life. Even if you feel you cannot do great things, said Mother Theresa, you can do small things with great love. She went on, "If you can't feed a hundred hungry people, then feed just one."

As the great British statesman Edmund Burke observed, "Nobody made a greater mistake than he who did nothing because he could only do a little."

Every parent has hundreds of chances to bring small expressions of love into the lives of their children. Sue Monk Kidd, author of *The Secret Life of Bees,* recalls the many ways her father creatively expressed his love for her. "He's the one who taught me to whistle, tie my shoes, ride a bike, love baseball and make pesto. The one who built my *stuffed* puppy an actual wooden doghouse, who came to my rescue when my kindergarten teacher criticized my penchant for coloring outside the lines, who labored patiently with me over math homework, and who drove me to weekend slumber parties."[6]

We might call these everyday gestures of caring "bits of hope" or "fragments of salvation." Too often we underestimate the power of a

---

6   Sue Monk Kidd & Ann Kidd Taylor. *Traveling with Pomegranates: A Mother-Daughter Story.* New York: Viking, 2009, p. 223.

touch, a smile, a kind word, a listening ear, an honest compliment, or a spontaneous act of caring, all of which have the potential to enrich and maybe even turn someone's life around.

It is perhaps in these simple acts of thoughtfulness that we show to each other day after day that we are especially God's gift to the world.

Just as the many trillions of cells in your physical body each do their little part to keep you healthy and developing, so each of the more than six billion people on our planet are the cells of humanity, each called to do their little part, to keep life on our planet healthy and developing. Unlike the cells in your body, which have little freedom to do anything but what they have been designed to do, we humans always have a choice in what we do or how we respond.

You turn on your faucet every day and trust that your water is safe to drink. Yet, almost 900 million people have no access to safe drinking water. Almost all of these live in developing countries. Over 3.5 million die each year from impure-water diseases. Statistically, every 15 seconds, a child dies from a water-related disease. An American taking a five-minute shower uses more water than a typical person in a developing country has access to in a day. And the water coming out of that shower nozzle is even safe to drink!

"In 2005, Tracy Hawkins from Atlanta, Georgia, took a three-week volunteer trip to teach pottery in Tanzania, saw the impact of unsafe drinking water, and has used her influence, her background in industrial engineering, and corporate America to change how this basic human need is met."[7]

She taught the Tanzanians how to make unglazed clay pots that serve as purifying filters. The local unsafe water is poured into the clay pots, this water seeps through the clay trapping parasites and bacteria, and out comes safe drinkable water, drop by drop.

You Are God's Gift in the Workplace

The most obvious place to begin making a difference is in your job. Look at your work with fresh eyes. "Realize your job is bigger than you think," says John Izzo, author of *Second Innocence: Rediscovering Joy and*

---

7   Nancy Hancock, *Spirit of Service: Your Daily Stimulus for Making a Difference*. San Francisco: HarperOne, 2009, p. 53.

Wonder. "Is it possible that whatever you are doing, your true work is deeper than you think? Believe it or not, you can save the world a little bit in every interaction you have and every role you play if you decide you want to. Rediscover the deeper purpose of your work. Each day ask, 'How can I make someone's day?'"

Most of us do our jobs as best we can, and in doing so we help change the balance of love and caring in the world.

Sanitation workers who carry off the smelly garbage we don't want, help keep disease from taking over a city.

Construction people will build safe and attractive houses and office buildings for us, even though they come home each evening with sore arms and aching backs.

People driving buses, cabs, trucks, trains and planes, spending long boring hours behind the wheel, continue to deliver people to where they want to go and goods to where you and I may need them.

Law enforcement officers and firefighters will risk their lives again and again to keep the rest of us safe.

Media people will inform and entertain. If you've ever watched a film through to the end credits, you will see long lists of behind-the-scenes people with unfathomable titles like "gaffer" and "best boy" that help make the movie or the television show a success.

On-call repair people with their hip-hanging tool belts help keep everything working in our homes, schools and offices.

Think of the salespeople, cashiers and customer service representatives who would like to walk away from or hang up on thoughtless and critical customers, but instead put on a smile, say a welcoming word and answer the same questions thousands of other have asked.

Schoolteachers continue to try to put ideas and information into resistant young minds, hoping at least to inspire them to learn and think. Teachers get little thanks for their efforts.

There are thousands of "invisible" workers who serve as janitors, housekeeping staff, maintenance workers and cleanup crews. Think of the crews at parks and stadiums who pick up aluminum cans, plastic bottles, crumpled paper, dropped food and spilled liquids that others thoughtlessly leave behind after a sports event or a concert.

These are a few of the positive differences people faithful to their calling can make, just by doing their daily jobs, even though they don't get much praise for it. All these and more are needed to keep the human family moving in the right direction and help renew the face of the Earth.

Small Positive Gestures

No matter where you happen to be, you can always give an affirmation instead of a putdown. You can always show patience instead of complaining. You can always take a deep breath instead of blowing your car horn in anger. You can always offer a helping hand instead of criticizing. You can try to find a way to reframe a bad situation instead of blaming someone for it. You can always step up and be helpful instead of remaining merely a curious bystander. In all of these cases, in adding a drop of hope, support, a little muscle or a bit of humor, you are helping to renew the face of the Earth.

One day, teenage John McCallister was bored, so his aunt handed him a copy of a *National Geographic* magazine to look at. For her, it was just a spontaneous gesture to distract the young man. But for him it was a transforming moment and a turning point. He went on to become a famous naturalist and horticulturist.

Nineteen-year-old Jane Goodall, without a college degree, wanted to study chimpanzees. After a public lecture she attended, the anthropologist James Leakey gave her a small word of encouragement. With that little word, she set off to Africa for a lifetime of study. During her 45 years there, she taught us more about the social life of chimps than any other anthropologist before or since.

A little black boy was sitting alone on a bench in an orphanage in New Orleans, when a counselor held up a trumpet and asked if he would like to play in the orphanage's band. That little boy's name was Louis Armstrong. If that man had not invited Louis to play, the most well known jazz musician in history may never have been seen or heard.

In this very basic sense of making a positive difference, every human person can contribute. As Mother Teresa reminded her Sisters, who served the poorest of the poor on the streets of Calcutta, "Let us always meet each other with a smile, for the smile is the beginning of love.

There are many in the world who are dying for a piece of bread, but there are many more dying for a little love."

Just by greeting people with a smile, a poor person may have as many opportunities in any given day to make a positive difference as a billionaire—and maybe more.

Poor people may have as many chances to be generous as those who are rich.

The sick may have as many chances of giving an affirmation as the healthy.

Older folk may have as many chances of offering help as the young.

The illiterate may have as many chances to show understanding as the highly educated.

Those in prison may have as many chances to show compassion as those of us who are free to come and go as we please.

Wherever you happen to be, give some time to care for your fellow humans. "Even if it's a little thing," wrote Albert Schweitzer, "do something for others—something for which you get no pay but the privilege of doing it." True generosity is doing something nice for someone who will never find out.

Donate a pint of your blood, volunteer at your local library, tutor a child or an adult immigrant learning English, welcome a foreign exchange student into your home for a semester, encourage your neighbors to vote, volunteer to work at your local animal shelter, visit a nursing home or a homebound neighbor, participate in a walk to support a cause like a cure for breast cancer, help a neighbor as he does his yard work, pick up trash you see on the sidewalk and dispose of it properly, find simple ways to beautify the earth you walk upon.

Those with little talent may have as many chances of being helpful as those with much talent, though from those with much talent and many resources, much more might be expected.

Unknown People Making a Difference for Us

Famous persons can make a positive difference, but so can those who are unknown. Think, for example, of computer programmers in their cramped cubicles who laboriously put together all those programs and applications that you call up many times a day on your computer or smart phone to make your life easier. Do you know the names of any one of these technicians? Probably not. They are among the many quiet and forgotten people who are helping renew the face of the Earth.

There are dozens of things in your life that make your life a bit more enjoyable or a bit safer.

How many times were you grateful that your car had windshield wiper blades, yet do you know who invented them?

You are grateful for nonglare headlamps on your vehicle—especially other vehicles—but do you know who invented them?

You are grateful to be able to buy canned goods at the supermarket, yet do you know who invented vacuum canning, that is, airtight food preservation?

You enjoy turning on your FM radio, but do you know who invented FM radio?

You may have enjoyed watching kids play with remote control toys like cars, boats and trucks, but do you know who invented wireless remote control that makes those toys work?

You enjoy watching color television, but do you know who invented the tricolor principle that made color television possible?

Do you know who was the inventor of one of the first electrically amplified acoustic guitars?

Do you know who is the father of the stem cell research that scientists say holds promise for the treatment of many diseases and ailments that currently defy cure?

Do you know the name of the engineer known as "the wizard of Sony" who created the precursor to the iPod, namely, the audiocassette and the Walkman that could play it?

(Answers to the above questions are given at the end of the chapter.)

This is not intended to be a quiz, but just a sample of how many people unknown to you have influenced your life.

To Praise or Not to Praise

Some among us will find their names mentioned and praised, while others make their contributions in the quiet background. When you go to a famous restaurant and enjoy a wonderful meal, you may give your compliments to the well-known chef. But how often have you given your compliments to the chef sweating behind the hot grill preparing your breakfast at Denny's, Perkins, Wendy's or McDonald's?

Many people make a difference in your life and the lives of others, yet receive little appreciation for their efforts. Getting praised for your caring gesture is a nice bonus, but not getting praised is no excuse for not making the caring gesture.

The gifts of some are widely recognized, those of others hardly noticed.

How many of us during a boringly long drive were saved by become engrossed in listening to a recording of a narrator reading a novel or other book as we drove? Yet how many of us have ever thanked Flo Gibson, the universally acknowledged *grande dame* of audiobooks. She entertained millions and shared her voice with listeners on over 1,134 books.

How many of us would know the name of Cyril M. Harris? He happened to be the acoustical engineer responsible for the beautiful sounds in many of the most prominent concert halls, theaters and auditoriums in the United States.

Do you know who discovered more chemical elements than any other human being? It was Albert Ghiorso, who died in 2011. He also designed many of the accelerators and detectors that made it possible for physicists to produce and identify the heavy, short-lived radioactive elements beyond uranium.

Do you know the name of the man who entertained generations of children by putting words into the mouths of Big Bird, Kermit the Frog and other characters on *Sesame Street*? It was Tony Geiss.

Do you know the name of the woman who inspired the first bill that President Barack Obama signed into law? Do you even know the name of the bill? Its title answers both questions: "The Lilly Ledbetter Fair Pay Restoration Act.

Lilly Ledbetter never set out to be a social pioneer. For nineteen years she worked at the Goodyear tire plant in Gadsden, Alabama, and was planning on taking an early retirement. One day, an anonymous note let her know that for years she had been paid less than her male co-workers for the same job. She took her wage discrimination case all the way to the Supreme Court, but lost it in a 5-4 decision. But she didn't give up. Lilly Ledbetter would not have other women suffer the injustice she did in her career.

President Obama commented when he signed that bill, "I sign this bill for my daughters, and all those who will come after us...In the end, that's why Lilly stayed the course. She knew it was too late for her—that this bill wouldn't undo the years of injustice she faced or restore the earnings she was denied. But this grandmother from Alabama kept on fighting, because she was thinking about the next generation. It's what we've always done in America—set our sights high for ourselves, but even higher for our children and grandchildren."

In 2010, two Russian-born scientists Andre Geim and Konstantin Novoselov shared the Nobel Prize in physics for groundbreaking experiments with a one-atom-thin material expected to play a large role in future electronics. The material is called graphene, a flake of carbon that is only one atom thick. No one had ever developed a material that thin; it's practically a two-dimensional reality. Since it's transparent and a good conductor, graphene is suitable for producing transparent touch screens, light panels and maybe even solar cells—definitely faster computers and innovative electronics. Their discovery has the potential to revolutionize the world of microelectronics for your children and grandchildren.

There are only a few who win a Nobel Prize or a Pulitzer Prize, but millions can win a smile or a quiet "Thank You" for their daily work and acts of kindness.

In the Holocaust Museum in Washington, DC, there is a list of "Righteous Gentiles" who willingly endangered their own lives to hide and save Jews from the Holocaust during World War II. That list is a reminder that there are many people, mostly those we don't know, who today will act with courage to make the world a better place.

Some people will make great breakthroughs with their gifts, while others will quietly comfort a brokenhearted widower, put a dollar in the hand of a homeless person, kiss and put a Band-Aid over the wound of a child who fell, or bake homemade cookies to make a boring meeting more enjoyable. God needs every last one of these people.

In the words of an Arabian proverb, "If you have much, give of your wealth; if you have little, give of your heart."

Many of us are afflicted with all-or-nothing thinking. If we can't write a check for a hundred dollars to a charity, we don't write one at all. If we can't spend an hour in a hospital room with a sick friend, we don't go at all. The problem with this "big" kind of thinking is that it denies the smallest comforts to those who need them the most.

Some gifts may take a certain person an entire lifetime to produce their effects, others will pour out many gifts in a short time. As far as anyone knows, Francis Scott Key wrote only one important song in his lifetime, The Star Spangled Banner; it became our national anthem. In contrast, Irving Berlin wrote over a hundred great songs, many of which were patriotic. We appreciate them both—for one gift or a hundred.

Some, like heroic soldiers on the battlefield, may lose their lives in bringing forth their gifts, while others, like wealthy philanthropists, may live in great comfort sharing their gifts. Nevertheless, all gifts given in love and compassion are fragments of salvation for the human race.

ANSWERS

Wiper blades: Mary Anderson (1866–1953) of the United States.

Nonglare headlamps: Turhan Alçelik (invented in 2006) of Turkey.

Vacuum canning: Nicolas Appert (1749–1841) of France.

FM radio: Edwin H. Armstrong (1890–1954) of the United States.

Wireless remote control: Robert Adler (1913–2007) of Austria.

Tricolor principle of color television: Hovannes Adamian (1879–1932) of Armenia.

Amplified acoustic guitar: Charles H. Kaman (1920-2011) of the United States. He was also an innovator in helicopter technology.

Father of stem cell research: Ernest A. McCulloch (1929-2011) of Canada.

Sony Walkman: Nobutoshi Kihara (1927-2011) of Japan.

Chapter 3

A Change in Perspective

For many centuries, people of faith, especially Christians, believed that Earth was little more than a testing ground for getting to heaven. They believed that God put them on Earth not to disturb things, but simply to avoid sin and thereby qualify for a heavenly mansion.

But today we are coming to understand more fully what God intended for humans when God created the universe. Thanks to science, we now know that our universe is close to 14 billion Earth-years old, that our planet Earth is a mere four billion years old, and that human culture as we know it has only been around about 100,000 years.

Scientists also generally agree today that our universe probably started off with a Big Bang, with trillions and trillions of elementary particles shooting off in all directions within a black cosmic void. Our telescopes show us, that after almost 14 billion years, the universe has self-organized into a vast array of billions of galaxies, and in each galaxy there are probably a billion suns (that we call stars), many with planets like our own orbiting around them (solar systems).

We like to think our Sun and our planet Earth are very special to God, because our planet started off as a spinning ball of red hot molten metals four billion years ago, and has come a long way in its evolutionary process to have spawned the complex forms of life we see today on Earth and in the human community.

But the first appearance of living forms on Earth took a long time. It was only after at least a billion years from Earth's beginnings that she produced forms of elementary life, like viruses, molds and bacteria. Over the next three billion years, these simple life forms eventually evolved into the many complex life forms that we know of today, such as plants, flowers, bushes and trees, insects and fish, birds and invertebrates, then in turn all kinds of mammals. Finally, after many trials and errors and much improvement, about 100,000 years ago, Earth gave birth to the very first creatures that could truly be called human beings. (Dinosaurs, by the way, died out 65 *million* years ago.)

When you grasp the immensity of God's creation and the many billions of years it took to make our planet ready to welcome its first human creatures, you begin to wonder: Why would God go through all this time and trouble if the only reason God wanted creation for was a place to give each human being a test to see if he or she qualified to graduate into heaven?

Doesn't it seem that God must have a larger plan in mind than that? Why spend 14 billion years and create billions of galaxies—and as many solar systems in each of the billions of galaxies—just to set up a simple qualifying test site for you and me? There must be something more in God's mind.

Once we accept the idea that God had something more in mind, we can begin to detect a divine plan evolving.

A Trajectory of Advancement

If we look at humanity's history over the last ten thousand years, we notice a certain trajectory of advancement happening. We observe tremendous and continuous improvements in transportation, technology, communication, education, medicine, commerce, culture, art, government, ethics and society. Everything seems to be evolving and bringing us closer to each other.

Because of those improvements in every field, we are making more and more connections among humans, life is growing more and more complex and unified, and it is forcing us to become more conscious and aware of ourselves and others than we have ever needed to be. From the isolated hunter-gatherer families and wandering tribes that characterized human social life many millennia ago, we are now a human community totally connected all over the planet. We enjoy almost instant communication with the other side of the globe and ever more rapid transportation. We have become, in effect, a seven-billion-member local community.

Think of the qualities of love and compassion, trust and forgiveness, creativity and innovation we need to invent, develop and produce in order for this one vast family to live and work together successfully and lovingly as one great social and spiritual organism!

One might say that this goal of "one great loving family" seems to be what God has been planning for us to achieve on Earth all along, that it has been God's plan to bring us together to learn how to love each other and become one cosmic body. It seems that God has implanted this divine project in our human hearts from the very beginning. Certainly Jesus' message was primarily about carrying out this divine project. "Thy will be done on Earth."

Christians throughout the centuries believed that this divine project was disclosed by Jesus and more broadly spelled out by St. Paul. Jesus' description of what God was doing in the world might be summarized in his prayer to God the Father:

"I ask not only on behalf of these [my apostles], but also on behalf of those who will believe in me through their word, that they may all be one. As you, Father, are in me and I am in you, may they also be in us, so that the world may believe that you have sent me. The glory that you have given me I have given them, so that they may be one, as we are one, I in them and you in me, that they may become completely one, so that the world may know that you have sent me and have loved them even as you have loved me." (John 17:20-23)

This oneness that Jesus talks about begins with service. People can learn to serve each other with love and compassion wherever they may be. It is loving and compassionate service that will help bring about this oneness.

To quote Martin Luther King, Jr. once again. "Everybody can be great. Because anybody can serve. You don't have to have a college degree to serve. You don't have to make your subject and your verb agree to serve.... You don't have to know the second theory of thermodynamics in physics to serve. You only need a heart full of grace. A soul generated by love."

"Unless someone like you cares a whole awful lot," wrote Dr. Seuss, "nothing is going to get better. It's not."

Dr. Seuss is talking about *you*. You are God's gift to the world. Your destiny is wrapped up in your "giftedness." Your challenge is to unwrap and open your gift, develop whatever abilities you find there, then use them to renew the Earth. Your assignment is to make life on Earth better in whatever little or large ways you can.

The first thing is to begin to notice the things in your neighborhood that need to be done that have been left undone.

Some organizations like to honor people who have made a difference in their community. For example, the American Society of News Editors (ASNE) regularly sponsors a Local Heroes event honoring individuals who fought tirelessly during the past year to make their state or local public institutions more open and accessible. Newspeople are interested in the freedom to access information and, in this case, the ability to access public records. In 2010, Suzanne Harris of Miramar Beach was recognized by ASNE in its national survey. She is a Florida woman whose lawsuit forced county officials to make significant changes in the way they handle public records. She is President of Edgewater Beach Condominiums Board of Directors.

Ms. Harris sued Walton County commissioners in October after receiving no response to her email requests for public documents containing certain key phrases. As a result of the lawsuit, the county agreed to a settlement. Because of it, Harris achieved a number of things: the commissioners agreed, first, to place the county under court scrutiny to comply with the state's Public Records Act; second, to hold annual training for public officials and key staff; third, to use only official county email accounts in its transactions; and, fourth, to designate an employee as a records management liaison officer.

When asked about why she sued the county, she replied, "The homeowners I represent were and are passionate about our private property rights, and we became even more passionate when the government intentionally and repeatedly violated our right to obtain the information that we needed to become informed. We sued to obtain redress for the government's infringement upon our private property rights." She added, "I hope my winning will show people that you have to hold local government accountable."

When asked what her message to others might be, she replied, "So often in life we encounter injustices and things that are just plain 'wrong.' All of us, myself included, often turn away and move on, reasoning that 'somebody else' will do something about it. If everyone thinks this way, then injustice and 'wrong' will prevail and become the norm. This cannot happen. If enough decent people are willing, when their times come, to step forward and be that 'somebody' who makes a difference in preventing an injustice and righting a wrong, then our communities and our families will be far to the better. Be that 'somebody else' when you see wrong and don't just walk on by."

Open Your Gift Completely

If you are God's gift to the world, it is important that you open up your gift completely. You may be surprised at the abilities and talents that may still be hidden inside you.

Little Lucy Larcom was born in Beverly, Massachusetts, in 1824, the ninth of ten children. She worked in the textile mill from age 11 to 21. As a mill girl she hoped to earn some extra money for her family. While working at the mills in Lowell, Lucy made a surprising discovery, that she had a gift for poetry and for writing. She wrote and published many of her songs, poems and letters describing her life at the mills. Her idealistic poems caught the attention of the famous poet John Greenleaf Whittier. Lucy Larcom's unsuspected talent made an impact on the world, and she served as a model for the change in women's roles in society. In one of her poems, she wrote:

If the world seems cold to you,
kindle fires to warm it.

The fact is we are, each of us, precisely God's gift to the world. God has given each of us to the world as a gift to "kindle fires to warm it"—to help transform it, enrich it, develop it, teach it and increase love, compassion, forgiveness, kindness, awareness and generosity among all people. In this way we can, indeed, become one in mind, one in spirit and one in love.

Whether you are a believer or an unbeliever, whether you are religious or not, whether you are spiritually minded or not, you are still God's gift to the world.

As the philosopher Leo Rosten remarked, "The purpose of life is not to be happy—but to *matter*, to be productive, to be useful, to have it make some difference that you have lived at all."

I know a young couple, who when their baby was born dead, planted a tree to bless the Earth and provide a haven for birds in memory of this child's life. For them, it was a way their child's life continues to make a small difference.

Beyond All Religions

The mystery of God's love and God's plan for evolving creation is beyond all religions, even though each religion may emphasize certain aspects of that plan. What is important is that God implants the law of love in your head, your heart and your genes. It's there, all right. It does not require some form of baptism, religious commitment or being born in the spirit to experience God's call. The inner call to make a difference—to *matter*—comes to absolutely everyone.

Norman Lear who grew up in a Jewish family in Connecticut had been a comedy writer for many famous sitcoms in the early days of television, including *All in the Family*, which won several Emmy Awards and remained the top-rated show on television for five consecutive years. His shows dealt with the political and social issues of the day, highlighting with humor some of the unjust prejudices very much alive in the United States of the 1970s. He went on to become a political activist and founded the civil liberties activist group *People for the American Way* in 1981. "It seems to me," he once said, "that any full grown, mature adult would have a desire to be responsible, to help where he can in a world that needs so very much, that threatens us so very much."

You do not have to profess a certain creed or assent to a set of doctrines to qualify to participate in the renewal of Earth. All you have to do is grow quiet and let yourself feel the wish to love and be loved, to feel that you are capable and competent to make a positive difference in your home, your workplace or your community.

Those who are believers, however, have no excuse. By their very profession of faith, they are called to stand in authentic presence to this truth about caring for our world and its people.

From an evolutionary perspective, each of the major world religions has given us its own unique perspective and emphasis on God and our relationship to God, specifically how we are to treat our fellow humans, other creatures and the Earth itself.

For example, Buddhist teachings emphasize compassionate caring for the weakest among us. Hindu teachings reflect awareness of the awesome power of divinity and the sacredness of all life, right down to the insects. Jewish teachings make us aware that God is among us, watching us, caring for us, guiding and protecting us—intimately involved in what we do to each other and to creation. The teachings of Islam remind us that each one must surrender one's total self to God and the work of God on Earth. Christian teachings emphasize the depth and breadth of God's love, and the command that we should be all-embracing in our love for one another. As one pastor put it to his Christian congregation, "You are committed to loving and caring for all others on our planet *precisely because you are a Christian*."

The Religious Expectation

Being a religious person may seem like a burden, rather than a privilege. For example, if you happen to be a Christian believer, you *know* what God is doing in the world and how you are expected to live a life of service. The same is true for every other major religion on Earth. Like all other believers, Christians have no excuse for "missing the point" of religion. It is all clearly spelled out in the New Testament's "good news" (or, in Old English, the "gospel").

One of the most famous gospel stories is the parable of the Good Samaritan. In the story, a Jewish man on a journey was attacked and beaten by robbers. Two Jewish holy men, a priest and a Levite, walked by—and even crossed to the other side of the road—to avoid having to deal with the wounded traveler. In contrast, a Samaritan businessman (At the time, Jews and Samaritans in general hated each other) saw the wounded Jew and felt compassion for him. The Samaritan cared for the victim, put him on his donkey, took him to an inn, paid for his care, and even promised, on his way back, to pay for any other expenses the victim may have incurred.

Commenting on this parable told by Jesus the Jew, the Rev. Martin

Luther King, Jr. said, "As each person saw the wounded Jew, he had to ask himself a question. The first question which the priest and the Levite asked was: 'If I stop to help this man, what will happen to me?' But the Good Samaritan reversed the question: 'If I do not stop to help this man, what will happen to him?'"

Did those who walked past the wounded man not feel the call to compassion? Of course they did. We all would. God built it into our very nature. But, like many of us, the priest and Levite had trained themselves to let that moment pass. Perhaps they said to themselves something like, "I'm too busy" or "Someone else will take care of him." And went on their way.

The Spirit of God

In Christian tradition, it is the role of the Holy Spirit of God to carry out the sacred transformation of humanity.

On the great feast of Pentecost, the day God's Holy Spirit gave birth to the Christian community, the believers were filled with God's Spirit and went forth to teach the world about what God was doing for our Earth and the people and creatures on it. Down through the centuries, Christians have continued to sing this hymn to God's Spirit.

Come, Holy Spirit, fill the hearts of Your faithful,
Enkindle in them the fire of Your love.
Send forth Your Spirit, and they shall be created,
And You shall renew the face of the earth.

God's love and God's divine plan for our vast universe transcend racial origin, sexual orientation or religious preference. Everyone is invited by God to help renew the face of the Earth. As the Buddha once said, "Thousands of candles can be lighted from a single candle, and the life of the candle will not be shortened. Happiness never decreases by being shared."

Everyone is capable, valuable and unique in God's plan. God can work through everyone and everything, every culture, every religion, every political system, every financial structure. Because God speaks directly to your listening heart, God is quite capable of using your talents, whoever you are and in whatever state of mind you happen to be.

Edward Everett Hale, Chaplain of the U.S. Senate early in the 20th century, was a forceful personality, an organizing genius and a practical theologian. For half a century he was active in raising the tone of American social and political life. He had a deep interest in the anti-slavery movement, education for all, and the workingman's home. In one of his speeches, he said,

I am only one,
but I am one.
I cannot do everything,
but I can do something.
And I will not let what I cannot do
interfere with what I can do.

The Un People

You are still God's gift to the world even though, in the eyes of others, you may happen to be unwanted, unwell, undocumented, untalented, uncredentialed, unemployed or unschooled. Even if you are old or handicapped.

The civil rights movement in the United States was sparked by the courageous actions of one rather ordinary African-American woman, Rosa Parks, who on December 1, 1955, in Montgomery, Alabama, refused to move to the back of the bus.

You are still God's gift to the world even though you feel lonely, downhearted, discouraged or depressed. Even if you are homeless, rejected, abandoned or persecuted. The desire to love and be loved is still alive in your soul. That desire is all you need to begin making a positive difference.

"The human race advances only by the extra achievements of the individual," said the politician Charles A. Towne. "And you are that individual."

You are still God's gift even though you may be diagnosed as addicted, ADD/ADHD, traumatized, mentally ill, chronically ill or terminally ill. By the way, these afflictions provide no reason for claiming you have little or nothing to contribute to God's grand plan. In God's world, no one gets a Handicapped Parking excuse. Everyone is able, not disabled.

Born blind and deaf, Helen Keller went on to earn a college degree and became a famous author, lecturer and political activist. She wrote, "The world is moved along, not only by the mighty shoves of its heroes, but also by the aggregate of tiny pushes of each honest worker."

Apathy and defeatism—the kind that can sometimes render individuals powerless to change things—are unacceptable in this divinely assigned job. "If you have time to whine and complain about something," Anthony J. D'Angelo advised students in his *The College Blue Book,* "then you have the time to do something about it."

Whether you are politically liberal or politically conservative, God wants your participation in the divine plan to transform the face of the Earth.

Whether you are humble or proud, an abuser or abused, a sycophant or a hypocrite, a pauper or a millionaire, it is still your destiny to be a part of God's plan.

Even if you have explored and tasted all of the seven deadly sins, you are still being called by God to participate in the renewal of the face of the Earth.

If you are ready to find and carry out what God wants you to do, begin observing closely some of the surprising events of your life.

Chapter 4

Coincidences and Miracles

Most people might define miracles as momentous and impressive results in the physical world that no human being could perform, such as instant healings from incurable diseases or unbelievable survival in a catastrophe. I wish to suggest a broader definition of "miracle," one that includes events where God's influence is, perhaps, a bit less spectacular.

Once you begin to acknowledge that you are God's gift to the world, you begin to make a big shift in how you perceive the seemingly trivial as well as the major events of your life. Especially events that many people dismiss as mere "coincidences." But you, as God's gift to the world, see these events differently because you realize that God's hand is always at work. Always.

God, you must remember, is present at every instant and in every place and in every human heart promoting the renewal of the face of the Earth. So, if you bump into someone you didn't expect to see, or you pick up a book whose title sends a message to you, or you arrive late for a meeting through no fault of your own (and discover you had avoided an accident because of your tardiness), you begin to learn to treat these coincidences as little miracles.

In the Preface to their book *Little Miracles II*, Yitta Halberstam and Judith Leventhal write (referring to individuals sometimes with a *he* and sometimes with a *she*):

> *When a person dismissively shrugs off a "coincidence" as merely a random event or pure happenstance, he is doing himself—and the universe—a grave disservice. He is failing to apprehend a divine moment that was gifted to him by God, a ripe and full moment*

that comes in the great flow of energy in which he is a spark. Had he recognized the coincidence for what it truly is—God's gentle tap on the shoulder or God's veritable shout: "Hello from heaven!"—his spark would have united with other scattered sparks and ignited into one giant flame. He would have entered a corridor into a different dimension, and his days and nights would have been illuminated by a brilliant light.[8]

A Life Full of Little Miracles

Helen Suruda, a personal friend for many years, died in her mid-nineties. She lived alone in St. Petersburg, Florida, on a very limited income. She never learned to drive, but rode her bicycle everywhere—to visit friends, to go shopping, to attend church services. What was special about Helen was that she found little miracles in her life every day. If a phone call came from a friend or a family member, she would see it as a small miracle. If a letter or a picture post card came from someone she knew, it was a little miracle. If a kitchen appliance that was on its last legs worked when she turned it on, it was a little miracle. If a rather expensive supermarket product she needed happen to be on sale that week, it was another blessing. Whenever someone telephoned her, she would always begin by listing the little miracles that had happened to her that day. As a Eucharistic minister for her church, she volunteered to bring Holy Communion to people in the hospital. Whenever she encountered a patient from Europe who spoke only Polish or Lithuanian, she would see it as a miracle that God had directed her to this bedside. She had spent many young years in Poland during World War II. Each of these small events reflected God's purpose to her and enabled her to live out her own unique purpose.

The authors of *Little Miracles* echo Helen's sentiments:

> *She will believe that the events in her life have purpose, that the "coincidences" in her life have purpose and that—most important of all—her very life is hallowed by sacred purpose. She will see the holiness*

---

8   *Small Miracles II: Heartwarming Gifts of Extraordinary Coincidences* by Yitta Halberstam and Judith Leventhal. Holbrook, MA: Adams Media Corp, 1998, pp. v-vi.

of day-to-day existence, the holiness of herself. And in a world where nihilistic forces threaten at times to submerge us, this is the greatest blessing of all.[9]

Making the Shift

Once we make this shift from "coincidences" to "miracles," we are forced to examine our lives more closely and we become more attentive to little surprising occurrences. As we develop a new sense of awareness about the "coincidences" that come into our lives, it fills us with excitement and gratitude. We begin to feel that we have truly been called to bring about God's kingdom on Earth, and that God is always with us. To quote again from *Little Miracles*:

> *Once you open your heart to 'coincidences,' these surprises begin flowing into your life. Moreover, you begin to examine your past with a different perspective and you may recognize that miracles have been happening around you all along. You 'simply hadn't identified them by their rightful name.*[10]

Musicians seem to find this shift from coincidences to miracles easier than others. The famous concert pianist Artur Rubenstein once remarked. "I have adopted the technique of living life miracle to miracle."

Eda J. LeShan, the famous child psychologist and consultant to the long-running children's television series *Sesame Street*, said, "A new baby is like the beginning of all things—wonder, hope, a dream of possibilities."

And the famous concert cellist and orchestral conductor, Pablo Casals, often told parents that they should recognize their child as a miracle, and they should often remind their child that he or she is a unique, unrepeatable miracle. Children need to hear this message until they truly recognize who they are. In his words, "The child must know that he is a miracle, that since the beginning of the world there hasn't

---

9   *Ibid.* p. vi.

10   *Ibid.* pp xi-xii.

been, and until the end of the world there will not be, another child like him."

How wonderful it would be if we all had a sense that we each were unique miracles given to the Earth as gifts of God! We are not to act as though, being God's gifts, we were entitled to see ourselves as kings and queens or somehow greater than the rest of the human race. We are simply gifts of God who go about every day and do something to make a positive difference.

Small Coincidences/Miracles are Often God's Call

God's call doesn't come only by God making face-to-face contact with you or in the quiet moments of prayer. God's "voice" may come in wherever and in whatever voice God may choose to be heard. God uses newspapers, books, magazines, radio and television—even commercials—as little miracles to surprise us and wake us up.

For example, God's call may come while you are watching television or listening to the radio. As theologian Patricia Sanchez noted, "When earthquakes, fires, mudslides, floods and famine are reported with all their sad and grim statistics, is it not the voice of God saying, 'There is need here. These are your brothers and sisters calling out to you. Can you hear my voice in their cries?'"[11]

Many of us tend to mute out television commercials or use them as time to grab a snack, but even those ads can sometimes be a little miracle, for example, when a commercial gives us an idea of how we can better serve.

A priest in our parish told us how his sermon about spiritual renewal was inspired by a television commercial for a woman's facial cream. The ad promised that if a woman used this facial cream faithfully, it would help clean, renew and revitalize the cells of her skin. In his sermon, the priest told the story of the television commercial, then made an analogy to what people could do to help clean, renew and revitalize their lives. If people were as committed to rejuvenating their spirits as much as they were about refreshing and renewing their skin, he said, it would transform the world. Now, I suspect that often when parishioners see

---

11   Patricia Datchuck Sanchez, "Calls and Echoes of Calls," *National Catholic Reporter*, January 7, 2011, p. 25.

a commercial for a women's facial cream, the point of that sermon is re-triggered in their minds.

Again Patricia Sanchez observes some very ordinary ways the voice of God comes to us.

> *Then there are the calls that come via telephone. This committee or that needs a leader; this project needs volunteers; someone needs a ride to the doctor, to the grocery store, to church. Do you have anything to offer a family made poor by unemployment? Can you make something for the bake sale? Can you help with this, with that? While all these in-between calls may seem unimportant or inconsequential compared with the real 'biggies' of life, it is in these small calls that disciples learn the faithfulness and sensitivity that will prepare them to recognize and respond to God's greater call when they come.[12]*

There is no such thing in anyone's life as an unimportant day.

God uses all the social media, like Facebook and Twitter. Beginning in January 2011, the political revolutions in the Near East, starting in Tunisia and Egypt, to bring freedom to oppressed people there were quickly organized. This was accomplished, miraculously, by people tapping out millions of messages to one another via smart phones and email. These social media allowed them to organize peacefully and powerfully. Enabling people to achieve freedom from oppression is always God's work.

---

12 *Ibid.*

Chapter 5

Everyone is Called, Absolutely Everyone!

In hospital delivery rooms all over the world, it has often been noted that, moments after a baby is born, the room, already bright with hospital lights, is filled with an unusually ethereal light and a sense of loving energy. Since the appearance of light and energy coincide with the emergence of the child from the mother's womb, people say it is the newborn's energy and love that fills the room. Everyone in the room feels it.

Perhaps this emanation of light and energy is God's way of saying to the parents and the hospital staff, "Here is another precious gift of life from me to the world. Take care of it. Teach it to love and help it to make its contribution to my plan for the world."

If God has a plan or project to be carried out on Earth and God invites all human beings to cooperate in this work, then it must be that every human being has an active role to play in this work.

God did not just invite Catholics or Protestants or Jews or Muslims or Buddhists or Hindus to participate in renewing the face of the Earth, but everyone, even nonbelievers and atheists. In fact, in some cases, it has been nonbelievers and atheists who have helped further God's work in many areas. For example, some atheist writers who have made a positive difference in the world include Mark Twain, Isaac Azimov, Dave Barry, Simone de Beauvoir, Daniel Dennett, Christopher Hitchens, and Salman Rushdie.

It is not required that you consciously know that you are cooperating in helping God's plan come to its fulfillment, only that you carry out your purpose in life. God's invitation is written in each person's heart as well as in their genes and in their experiences and culture.

While religious beliefs may help many in discerning or encouraging one's vocation to serve, even the atheist will feel an inner call to excel in a certain area and make a contribution to human growth and development.

Once you understand what it is that God is trying to accomplish in the world and consider how you could contribute to it, you have little excuse for avoiding a willingness to cooperate.

Many of us in the Western World will do whatever we can to avoid getting involved in something that might make us feel "uncomfortable." So, many of us feel entitled to a free ride, counting on the work and effort of others without doing our share. In the words of animal rights activist Jane Goodall, "The greatest danger to our future is apathy."

There are many wonderful examples of people who, despite their handicaps—physical, mental or emotional—made their contributions.

People with Mental and Emotional Problems

Petite little Temple Grandin didn't speak until she was almost four years old. All she could do was scream and hum. In 1950 she was labeled "autistic," and doctors recommended she be institutionalized. Experts in those days believed that autistic persons had no inner life. But Temple proved them wrong. Her parents didn't believe the doctors. Although communication was difficult for her as she grew up, she went on to finish college and even completed her doctorate. Today, Dr. Temple Grandin, though she remains an adult with autism, is recognized as a foremost authority on designing equipment for humane handling of livestock. It seems a strange vocation for a young woman, but it turned out to make a lot of sense.

Remembering her years as an autistic child unable to communicate with others, she could empathize with animals that couldn't communicate their feelings to humans. She especially noticed the fear building up in cattle in the slaughterhouse. After all, the cows could see and hear the dying cries of the other cattle. To lessen their fear—even though she could not stop the beef business—she designed the slaughterhouse ramps as compassionately as possible so that the cattle could not see or hear those on the ramp ahead of them being slaughtered. Today, almost half of the country's livestock facilities and slaughterhouse ramps in use were designed by her.

More importantly, by her accomplishments she has transformed the way psychiatrists and psychologists think about the possibilities for people with autism to make a difference in the world.

Albert Einstein, perhaps the most famous physicist of the 20th century and winner of the Nobel Prize in Physics, showed classic symptoms of autism. People say Einstein could not speak before the age of four, and even at nine he could not speak fluently. Language delays are common in children with high functioning autism. His parents suspected that he might actually be mentally retarded. Children and adults with autism and Asperger's Syndrome, a form of autism, often have peculiar habits and extreme sensitivity to textures. Einstein was often seen demonstrating odd behaviors, and seemingly lost in his own world. For example, at his ceremony of induction as an American citizen, Einstein attended in suit and tie, but forgot to put on socks.

Despite their sometimes lack of social skills, conversational skills, strange speech patterns, preoccupation in a particular area of interest and lack of normal emotional control, many persons with autism manage to make a great difference in the world.

Because many autistic people tend to focus on one thing, they can often master a field more quickly than others. For example, Tim Ellis became a famous Australian magician; Jerry Newport became a mathematical savant; Tim Page became a Pulitzer Prize-winning author; many, like Satoshi Tajiri, creator and designer of Pokémon, become computer experts; some, like Matt Savage, become musical prodigies.

Among the most common cortical brain area disabilities today are *ADD (Attention Deficit Disorder)* and *ADHD (Attention Deficit Hyperactivity Disorder)*. People with either of these disorders are often plagued with inattentiveness, over-activity and impulsivity. People with ADHD symptoms often put stress on life in a family.

Most children with ADHD also are afflicted with at least one other developmental or behavioral problem. Such people, we might think, have a good excuse for not being committed to making a positive difference in the world. Yet, many have turned this mental and behavioral affliction to good use.

Some well known people who have been diagnosed with ADD/ADHD and have made a significant contribution include: actor Jim Carrey, football quarterback Terry Bradshaw, singer-actress Cher, comedian and actor Bill Cosby, actor Tom Cruise, actress Whoopi Goldberg, basketball star "Magic" Johnson, musician John Lennon, filmmaker Steven Spielberg, comedian Robin Williams and musician Stevie Wonder.

Another developmental disorder that afflicts many is *dyslexia*, usually manifested as a reading disability when a person cannot properly process words on a page. Dyslexia is a developmental disorder, not a mental deficiency. Most people with dyslexia have normal intelligence or above normal intelligence. However, dyslexia is debilitating, since so much of human communication, learning and formal education is done through written words.

It is surprising how many people, despite being afflicted with this disorder, have accomplished great things. Here are just a few who are dyslexic or manifest traits associated with dyslexia or related learning styles: Carol Greider, molecular biologist, awarded the 2009 Nobel Prize in Medicine; statesman and president John F. Kennedy; entertainer and talk show host Jay Leno; designer Tommy Hilfiger; cartoonist of *Dilbert* Scott Adams; John T. Chambers, CEO of computer parts giant Cisco Systems; William Hewlett, co-founder of computer manufacturer Hewlett-Packard; Paul J. Orfaleas, founder of Kinko's; and financial investor Charles Schwab.

People with Physical Disabilities and Chronic Pain

Frida Kahlo (1907-1954) was a famous Mexican painter, perhaps best known for her self-portraits. Kahlo's work is remembered for its "pain and passion" and its intense, vibrant colors. Her work has been celebrated by Mexicans as promoting national tradition, and by feminists for its uncompromising depiction of the female experience and form. Those who have merely admired her paintings in art museums and are probably unaware of the emotional burdens and physical pains she bore throughout her life

Kahlo contracted polio at age six, which left her right leg thinner than the left. Kahlo disguised this by wearing long, colorful skirts. She also suffered from spina bifida, a congenital disease that affected both her spinal and leg development.

When she was eighteen, Kahlo was riding in a bus when the vehicle collided with a trolley car. She suffered serious injuries in the accident, including a broken spinal column, a broken collarbone, broken ribs, a broken pelvis, eleven fractures in her right leg, a crushed and dislocated right foot, and a dislocated shoulder. An iron handrail pierced her abdomen and her uterus, which seriously damaged her reproductive ability.

For many months, she had to lie in bed on her back. She had her parents put a mirror on the ceiling over her bed. In that position, Kahlo began a full-time painting career, while she recovered in a full body cast. Immobilized, she painted to occupy her time. Her self-portraits became a dominant part of her life during recuperation. Kahlo once said, "I paint myself because I am so often alone and because I am the subject I know best." Her mother had a special easel made for her so she could paint in bed, and her father lent her his box of oil paints and some brushes.

Although she recovered from her injuries and eventually regained her ability to walk, she was plagued by relapses of extreme pain for the remainder of her life. The pain was intense and often left her confined to a hospital or bedridden for months at a time. She underwent as many as thirty-five operations as a result of the accident, mainly on her back, her right leg and her right foot.

Drawing on personal experiences, including her marriage, her miscarriages, and her numerous operations, Kahlo's works, on display in many art museums, often are characterized by their stark portrayals of pain. Of her 143 paintings, 55 are self-portraits, which often embody symbolic portrayals of physical and psychological wounds. She insisted, "I never painted dreams. I painted my own reality."

Tom Shadyac was the biggest comedy director in Hollywood. His hits, including "Ace Ventura: Pet Detective," "The Nutty Professor," "Liar, Liar," and "Bruce Almighty," grossed more than a billion dollars. In October, 2010, his handmade film called "I Am" premiered. In addressing the audience before the screening, he said he hoped that this film, unlike his others, would change the world. "I Am" emerged from a new awareness of life that came after a tumble from a bicycle in 2007, "that led to a post-concussive infirmity so severe that he began…to canvass the world for meaning."[13] To a *New Yorker* interviewer, Shadyac said, "I think the bike accident knocked me into my heart." The new film describes his personal story of conversion.

His movie's point is "to suggest that the natural world is deeply interconnected—and that we are by nature cooperative, that markets don't measure our value, and that the heart, not the brain, is our primary organ."

As part of his decision to change the world, Shadyac gave up his private jet—and cell phone. He sold his mansion/compound in Pasadena and moved into a trailer park in Malibu. He has built a shelter for the homeless and has funded the rescue of African child soldiers. At present, he is touring the country, often by bicycle, to promote his film.

Shadyac's father, Richard, a lawyer and top executive at St. Jude Children's Research Hospital in Memphis, died before the film was complete. But Tom did interview his father while making the film. In the interview, Tom asked his father, "Is it possible to build a business where we don't leave our principles at the church door?" and the father replies, "No, not knowing [the heart of] man."

Shadyac said that his father epitomizes our cultural sickness. With all my father did in managing the building of that most beautiful hospital, he was "still stuck inside the sack of our culture," having little hope for humanity's potential future.

Shadyac hopes his film will split this cultural sack wide open, allowing us to stick our heads out and see what is truly there, and show us that, together, we can change the world.

Christopher Reeve (1952 –2004) was an American actor, film director, producer, screenwriter and author. He achieved stardom for his acting achievements, including his notable motion picture portrayal of the fictional superhero Superman.

On May 27, 1995, Reeve became a quadriplegic after being thrown from a horse in an equestrian competition in Virginia. He required a wheelchair and breathing apparatus for the rest of his life. Instead of

---

13 This and the following quotations are from Tad Friend, "The Pictures: Detour" in *The New Yorker*, November 15, 2010, p. 35-36.

giving up or despairing, he lobbied on behalf of people with spinal cord injuries, and for human embryonic stem cell research. He founded the Christopher Reeve Foundation and co-founded the Reeve-Irvine Research Center. As he put it, "The fact is that even if your body doesn't work the way it used to, the heart and the mind and the spirit are not diminished. It's as simple as that."

Franklin Delano Roosevelt, one of the greatest presidents of the United States, guided America successfully through the Great Depression and through most of World War II. And he did it strapped to a wheelchair, a survivor of the polio epidemic that swept through America for more than twenty years. He contracted polio in 1921 at the age of 39. Thus, Roosevelt, a public figure, was faced with the greatest struggle of his life—to triumph over his disability. In those days, things were different. If you had a disability, you kept it secret as much as possible. It was not to be spoken of, nor were you to display it in public. Sensitive to these attitudes both at home and abroad, he often kept his disability hidden.

Winston Churchill also knew of Roosevelt's successful struggle with this illness. In a speech to the House of Commons, Churchill said that even with his disability, Roosevelt had become "the indomitable master of the scene."

Roosevelt responded to his disability not by reducing his life efforts or going into seclusion. Instead, he remained in politics at the highest levels. He embraced all the risks the greater world had to offer. Just as he challenged himself to triumph over his adversity, his example challenged the world—and all of us—to triumph over adversities such as war, poverty and hatred. From his wheelchair he not only inspired the world, he transformed it for the better.

Some other *physically handicapped people* who have helped change the world include: Jane Addams, advocate for the poor and founder of Hull House; Charles Steinmetz, electrical engineer and member of the board of education, committed to helping all students from the retarded and autistic to the bright and eager; William O. Douglas, member of the United States Supreme Court, who suffered from polio; Gustav Mahler, famous German composer of symphonies; crippled Henri Toulouse-Lautrec, French Impressionist painter; William James, author and early psychological researcher into spirituality, suffered from spinal problem, digestive problems, eye trouble and frequent bouts of deep depression; Ring Lardner, writer and poet, wore braces all his life because of a misshapen foot; Eleanor Roosevelt, the president's wife, a pro-labor advocate, lived with spinal problems all her life; as did the famous composer Bela Bartok. Not only did these people overcome the challenge of their disabilities, they challenged the way we often think about those with disabilities.

Among those who made a difference despite *serious eye disorders or very poor eyesight* include: British poet Rudyard Kipling, writer Aldous Huxley, Irish playwright Sean O'Casey, United Nations statesman Syngman Rhee, American President Harry S Truman, Chief Justice of the Supreme Court Louis Brandeis, writer Emile Zola, novelist James Joyce, and poet Carl Sandburg.

Many other well known people who have made a positive difference—the list is too long to print—include those who came from troubled homes, broken homes, poor homes, alcoholic parents, drug addicted parents, physically abusive parents, sexually abusive parents or divorced parents, Others did not know their fathers, or even their mothers. Some ran away from home or got in trouble with the law or were severely overweight. Yet, somehow they all managed not merely to survive but to make a positive difference with their lives.

People Born into Poverty

Our times are filled with people who grew up in poverty and managed to make major positive improvements in the quality of our human lives. Let's look at some very well known figures.

Steve Jobs, co-founder of Apple Computer, is one of the most famous individuals in this category, along with Bill Gates. If you want to see how Jobs and his company have transformed the ways we communicate, just think of the desktop computer, the computer mouse, the pull down options on the tool bar (long before Windows), the iPod, iPhone and iPad. An orphan, Steve Jobs was adopted by a working-class couple and grew up in Santa Clara, California. He dropped out of Reed College when he couldn't afford tuition but continued auditing classes. Jobs started Apple Computer in his parents' garage in 1976. He left Apple for a while, but stayed busy managing Pixar, the biggest revolution in film animation since Disney. He returned to Apple 1996, but took leave of absence for a liver transplant. Later, he was back leading Apple's expansion in music and media through devices and software including iTunes.

Larry Ellison is the man behind the success of Oracle Software Company. His single teenage mother gave birth to Ellison in the Bronx, but sent him to live in Chicago with his aunt and uncle, who later adopted him. He dropped out of college after his adoptive mother died. He founded Oracle in 1977, which is now one of the world's biggest software companies. Chances are you have Oracle programs working for you in your computer. Oracle probably has the most complete, open and integrated business software on the market.

You probably never associated the name Guy Laliberté with the popular show Cirque du Soleil. He is its founder. Guy was an acrobat showman. He began as a penniless, stilt-walking, fire-eating street performer in Paris. In 1984, along with some of his pavement exhibitionist pals, he started what has evolved into Cirque du Soleil. For the first seven years they barely made ends meet, but finally hit it big when they appeared in Las Vegas in 1991. Since then Cirque has expanded shows to include many different themes, delighting millions of people and demonstrating the incredible physical capacities and skills of the human person. On the side, Laliberté has become a poker champ.

Everyone knows J. K. Rowling as the author of the Harry Potter books and movie series. Today she is a billionaire, but while writing her books she was a single mother living on welfare in Edinburgh, Scotland. Broke and depressed, Rowling once told reporters she contemplated suicide. A significant part of her contribution to the renewal of the Earth came because her books motivated millions of children to become proficient readers. Her characters also showed young people how to nurture healthy friendships and mutual trust in one another.

Oprah Winfrey, queen of daytime talk shows, was born to a single teenage mother and raised by her grandmother on a farm. She was a victim of child sexual abuse. After her television talk show's phenomenal success, she started her on studio, published *O Magazine*, and launched her own Oprah Winfrey Network (OWN) cable channel.

Madame C. J. Walker (1867-1919), an African-American, grew up in Mississippi as the impoverished daughter of slaves. After working for a time as a laundress, she developed the first commercially successful hair-straightening process, known as the "Walker System." In her own words, "I am a woman who came from the cotton fields of the South. From there I was promoted to the washtub. From there I was promoted to the cook kitchen. And from there I promoted myself into the business of manufacturing hair goods and preparations. I have built my own factory on my own ground." By 1910, her company employed over three thousand people, and she was probably the first African-American woman to become a millionaire. Walker also became a patron of black writers and artists and established scholarships for African-American women at Tuskegee Institute. Her advice to us, "Don't sit down and wait for the opportunities to come; you have to get up and make them."

You can probably think of some other reasons why you should be excused from helping renew the face of the Earth, but for every excuse you conjure up you can find many others who had every right to use that same excuse, but didn't.

As the great heavyweight boxing champion Mohammed Ali cleverly but accurately described it, "Service to others is the rent you pay for your room here on earth."

Part II:

PRAYING

As One Who is God's Gift to the World

Chapter 6

Fundamental Choices

I f you are willing to accept yourself as God's gift to the world, and you can accept that you are an irreplaceable part of God's plan to renew the face of the Earth, then you will want to ground yourself in that work. Part of that work is making choices, not only in daily life but in prayer.

Making Choices

Someone once said that you just have to look at your choices in life to see who you are and discover your passion. Sue Sword, who has spent much of her life serving the poor in Appalachia, said: "Everyone is made up of choices, from the smallest choices, such as getting out of bed, to the biggest choices, such as whom you will marry. These choices lead us down a certain path, one that we would not have travelled if we had not made that choice. It is not the path itself or where it leads that defines us, but it was the decision to take that road."[14]

The most important thing to remember about making choices is that nothing really happens—nothing is changed—until we actually choose. For instance, suppose you go to a department store with the intention of buying a suit. You may try on many different suits. You may like a number of them. But, so far, nothing in your life has changed. You still have not done what you came to the store to do. *Buy a suit.* It is only when you have selected a specific suit, taken it to the cashier and paid for it that you have truly made a choice.

Choice alone releases the energy to accomplish or do something.

---

14 Sue Sword with Candace Delona Sword, *Sue's Memories of Home.* Hagerhill KY: Christian Appalachian Project, 2011, pp. 6-7.

Wishing for something or fantasizing about something is very different from actively choosing it and, thereby, releasing the energy to accomplish or acquire what you choose.

Once you can acknowledge that you are one of God's gifts to the world, you will be ready to offer each day a Fundamental Choice Prayer like the one below.

Fundamental Choice Prayer

Dear God,
I choose to live this day
as an instrument of your love and work in the world.
I choose to commit myself to your divine project,
whose goal is to bring all human persons together
into one great loving union.
Therefore,
I choose to live this day as healthily as I can
in body, mind and spirit.
I choose to live this day true to myself.
I choose to live this day to my personal best.
I choose to live this day taking responsibility
for making my contribution to the world.
Amen.

You may write this prayer out and paste it on your refrigerator or on a mirror in your bedroom or bathroom, so that you remember to make it consciously every morning. At night, you may want to review your day by identifying your contributions.

Practice Making Choices

It is important to practice making choices, to develop your skill in using your God-given gifts of free will and the ability to choose. It is recommended that each day you practice using this uniquely human way of releasing energy by making four Fundamental Choices. These are choices so basic to a healthy and creative life that every person can make them every day. Consider them as a basic spiritual practice. For example, you could reflect each day on how they can be lived out and acted upon during that day. Here are the four that are expressed in the prayer above.

Four Daily Fundamental Choices

1. I choose to live this day as healthily as I can—body, mind and spirit.

2. I choose to live this day true to myself.

3. I choose to live this day to my personal best.

4. I choose to live this day taking responsibility for making my contribution to the world.

These four choices offer a way to live consciously an optimally functional life.[15] Once you are grounded in these Fundamental Choices, you will be ready to create what you need to create to carry out your calling. Also these choices will ensure that what you create will be helpful in renewing the face of the Earth. They will help to maximize *you* as well as your potential to make a difference.

Each one is discussed here in turn.

The First Fundamental Choice

I choose to live this day as healthily as I can—body, mind and spirit.

Physical Health

The Chinese American actor Bruce Lee, famous for his Kung Fu movies, was a sickly child. Early on, Bruce Lee made what was a Fundamental Choice to develop his health. To do this, he turned to the martial arts and bodybuilding. Day after day, building up his physical health was a primary preoccupation, so much so that he became a

---

15   Robert Fritz, *The Path of Least Resistance: Learning to Become the Creative Force in Your Own Life.* New York: Random House, 1984. I learned these four fundamental choices while helping edit Fritz' book, and have been using them even since.

master of many martial arts and appeared in many movies. Bruce Lee shows the power of a person who makes this first Fundamental Choice for health.

The Frenchman Jacques Cousteau, the master of underwater photography and film, was quite sickly as a child. He too, in effect, made a Fundamental Choice for his health, but he did it, not with martial arts as Bruce Lee did, but by swimming. He learned to swim at the age of four. His initial dip in the water led to his everlasting love for the sea. Remaining true to the first Fundamental Choice turned him into a healthy man. He was also very curious about machines. At the age of 13, Cousteau saved his pocket money to buy a movie camera. The rest of his famous career in deepsea documentary films is history.

You can make this first Fundamental Choice no matter how sick or healthy you happen to be at the moment. Even a person with terminal cancer or a debilitating chronic disease can choose to live today as healthily as possible. My wife, a therapist, tells me of a woman patient who had a rare disease and, by her doctor, had been given four weeks to live. The patient made this first Fundamental Choice each morning and acted on it, physically, emotionally and spiritually. Her doctors were amazed, because the woman lived four more years.

Even the most vitally healthy person needs to make this choice, since the temptations to violate it are all around us every day.

"Take care of your body. It's the only place you have to live," says Jim Rohn, a motivational speaker whose own life is a wonderful rags-to-riches story.

Psychological Health

Perhaps the parts of this first Fundamental Choice that have to do with psychological health and spiritual health need a bit more emphasis, since we seldom think of the need to continually develop these parts of us.

On the psychological dimension, we can daily make the choice to do things that nurture intellectual development as well as self-confidence and healthy self-esteem. We can also learn how to deal with negative emotions, such as fear and anger. Living with the burden of poor self-esteem or being ruled by anxiety or fear can keep you from being God's gift to the world in ways you could be.

Psychologist Susan Jeffers, author of *Feel the Fear And Do It Anyway*, knew how debilitating fear could be. All through her life she heard inner voices—and, sometimes, outer voices—telling her: "You'd better not make a change. There's nothing else out there for you. You'll never make it on your own. Don't take chances. Be careful. You might make a mistake. And you'll be sorry."

Dr. Jeffers learned that it was her own thinking that kept her a prisoner of her fears. One day it occurred to her that she could *unlearn* self-defeating habits she had learned. She taught herself to unravel the complexities of fear. As she tells her students at the university, "I'm not promising that change is easy. It takes courage to mold your life the way you want it to be."[16]

Anger, like fear, can be debilitating, especially when you nurture it and keep it boiling. Remember, Every sixty seconds you spend angry, upset or mad, is a full minute of peace and happiness you'll never get back.

"You cannot control what happens to you," advises guru Sri Ram, "but you can control your attitude toward what happens to you, and in that, you will be mastering change rather than allowing it to master you."

For example, to create more positive results in your life, especially after a failure, replace the attitude "if only I had done this" with "I'll do better next time." A wise young man told me that failure happens only when you quit trying.

Spiritual Health

People are quite familiar with mental health, but some wonder what spiritual health means. It simply means having a healthy and vibrant human spirit. A healthy spirit is not the same as being "religious" or "devout," though for many people those qualities may be elements of a healthy human spirit.

Other qualities of a healthy human spirit include *creativity, courage,*

---

16   Susan Jeffers. *Feel the Fear and Do it Anyway.* New York: Fawcett Books, 1987, p. 6.

compassion, joy, faith, trust, hope, the ability to forgive, determination, wisdom, discernment and a loving heart. If some of these qualities are functioning well in your life, you are probably spiritually healthy. Notice that these spiritual energies are different from psychological emotions such as sadness, happiness, annoyance, frustration, fear, anger or excitement.

For example, joy is an often forgotten spiritual capacity. It is an emotion that is far deeper than "having fun" or "being happy." Rather, joy is the ability to see the beauty and depth of life, even when you are not having fun or feeling happy. Joy is the deep inner contentment you experience when you are doing what you were meant to do.

When James A. Garfield was President of the United States, he said, "If wrinkles must be written upon our brow, let them not be written upon the heart. The spirit should not grow old."

Gratitude is another very powerful spiritual energy. So, embrace gratitude. Be grateful for everything good you experience today, and say "thanks" also for what you have learned from your mistakes.

Never forget to express gratitude to people who seldom hear a word of thanks—like clerks, salespeople, ticket-takers, supermarket cashiers and the like. Don't just mutter the word "thanks." Give your gratitude some specificity. Thank people for their effort, their smile, their patience, their neatness, their efficiency, their special touch. Let the people who've touched you know how grateful you feel towards them. You'll be surprised what a simple expression of thanks can do, especially if it is tied to something specific about them you have felt or observed. If you don't tell people what they mean to you or how they have impacted your life, they'll probably never know.

Having goals to accomplish is usually seen as a quality of the human spirit. The human spirit likes to envision something to accomplish and to accomplish it. Greg Anderson, a personal fitness trainer, hit it on the button when he said, "When we are motivated by goals that have deep meaning, by dreams that need completion, by pure love that needs expressing, then we truly live life."

All these ideas are part of the Fundamental Choice to live this day as healthily as possible, body, mind and spirit.

The Second Fundamental Choice

I choose to live this day true to myself.

One day a woman came to the famous Indian spiritual leader Mohandas Gandhi with her overweight son in tow. She said, "My son won't give up eating sweets. Please tell him to stop. He will listen to you."

Gandhi looked at the boy and his mother and told them to come back in one week. Seven days later, the woman again approached the great man with her son. Gandhi said to the boy, "Please do not eat any more sweets."

The woman thanked Gandhi, then asked, "We have had such a long walk, Bapu. Why did you not tell him this a week ago?"

Gandhi answered, "Because a week ago I was still eating sweets."[17]

Gandhi worked on the principle, "My life is my message."

When we tell people to do things, as Gandhi did to this young boy, whether it's our children, our friends or our employees, it's essential to do so in a compassionate way. Gandhi felt it was impossible to ask someone to do something like give up eating sweets, unless he knew what he was asking for based on firsthand experience.

Every moment of life you get to spend is a gift. Spend it on things that matter. Spend it on things that make you feel true to your self.

"Everyone has his own specific vocation or mission in life," said Viktor Frankl, who survived years in a Nazi concentration camp during World War II. "In that calling he cannot be replaced, nor can his life be repeated. Thus, everyone's task is as unique as is his specific opportunity to implement it."

The Buddha reminds us that it takes effort to discover your true calling in life. "Your work is to discover *your* work and then, with all your heart, to give yourself to it."

Steve Jobs, the founder of Apple Computers and creator of a string of groundbreaking inventions, knows what it means to have a limited time to accomplish one's true purpose in life. He was a man beset by sickness. He had gone through a liver transplant and had been valiantly fighting pancreatic cancer, one of the most virulent cancers, for years.

---

17 *Spirit of Service.* p. 201.

His advice: "Your time is limited, so don't waste it living someone else's life…. Don't let the noise of others' opinions drown out your own inner voice. And most importantly, have the courage to follow your heart and intuition, for they somehow already know what you truly want to become. Everything else is secondary."

Steve Jobs changed the world of social media and electronic communication. That was his gift. Each of us is called upon by God to make a difference in the lives of others in whatever way we were meant to. To live up to who you truly are, you may need to change the way you think about yourself.

Because you are unique, you are exceptional. Realizing that truth may help you achieve surprising success on the job, on the playing field, or in any situation that demands you rise above and beyond what you ever thought possible.

Inspirational teacher John Eliot points out, "History shows us that the people who end up changing the world—the great political, social, scientific, technological, artistic, even sports revolutionaries—are always considered nuts, until they are discovered to be right. And then they are called geniuses."

John Eliot believed everyone had the potential to be a genius in some field or other, except that most people are afraid of living up to their potential.

"Remembering you are going to die," said Steve Jobs who had been facing death for a number of years, "is the best way I know to avoid the trap of thinking you have something to lose. You are already naked. There is no reason not to follow your heart."

To be true to yourself, says Howard Thurman, do the things that make you feel truly alive. Most people look around to see what is needed, then they go and fill that need. Howard Thurman took a different approach to being true to yourself. "Don't ask yourself what the world needs, ask yourself what makes you come alive. And then go and do that. Because what the world needs is people who are alive."

Howard Thurman, an influential American black author and educator, died in 1981. He left his position as dean of Howard University, with its almost exclusively black faculty and student body, because he felt that racial integration was not happening fast enough in the United States. Working for integration was what made him feel fully alive. So, being true to himself, he moved to San Francisco and co-founded the first, fully integrated, multi-cultural church in America. His work for integration was what gave him life. If you have some activity that makes you feel truly alive, that brings you deep joy, you can be sure it is part of God's plan.

The Third Fundamental Choice

I choose to live this day to my personal best.

There are always to be found those who represent everything that truly is good about our community, our nation and our world. They feel an inner call to do good to improve the conditions in which people live.

At age 8, Evangeline Best, a pretty African-American girl, started her career of service by cleaning up the streets of East Tampa where she lived. Each morning, she would go out on her street and pick up debris that was left on the sidewalks and in gutters from the night before. Now 67, she's still there, redeveloping and revitalizing that same neighborhood through her efforts with the Corporation to Develop Communities of Tampa. "I don't know nothing else," she said. "I know I have to do it."

Currently, Evangeline teaches job and life skills to youth, works with community leaders to make East Tampa safer, and she champions race relations. And her volunteer work does not go unnoticed. Recently, she won recognition as a "local hero" from Bank of America, collecting a $5,000 prize to donate back to the CDC, where she serves on its board. "Today, I'm standing on the stage. I think it tells you I'm here because I believe in what I can do."[18]

Living to our best often requires major choices. "Change will not come if we wait for some other person or some other time," said President Barack Obama. "We are the ones we've been waiting for. We are the change that we seek."

We stand on the shoulders of people who have gone before us being the best they can be. But now we are the ones who have the chance to

---

18 Story from Stephanie Wang, "Best of 'local heroes' feted at Oscars-style ceremony," *St. Petersburg Times*, Friday, November 12, 2010.

create the future. The philosopher Herbert Spencer put it this way, "The wise man must remember that while he is a descendant of the past, he is a parent of the future."

And if we are to create the future, we should not have small or mediocre plans for humanity and the rest of God's creation, but great plans. Only our personal best will do.

What are you planning to do today that will show that you have chosen to live up to your personal best? As Robin Sharma says, "The smallest of actions is always better than the noblest of intentions." Let your acts reflect your Fundamental Choice to live to your personal best. Turn your good intentions into actions.

The Fourth Fundamental Choice

I choose to live this day taking responsibility for making a difference in the world.

Today, Reverend James Coleman is in the business of giving hope. Before today, Coleman spent seven and a half years behind bars for armed robbery to support a crack habit. Like others, when he got out he couldn't find a job. So, at his local church he volunteered to do cooking, serving food and helping others. He finally discovered what he wanted to create. He developed the Over Comers Support Group for ex-offenders, which meets regularly. He says at least half of the people he works with find some form of success.[19]

Are you an ex-offender or were you born in dire poverty? It doesn't make any difference. You can still take responsibility for figuring out and then creating the life purpose that God gave you.

Jim Rohn is a man who started life out in rags, but now is a wealthy entrepreneur. For his purpose in life, he has taken responsibility for helping others create the life that they want. "If you don't design your own life plan," he says, "chances are you'll fall into someone else's plan. And guess what they have planned for you? Not much."

If you have not taken responsibility for your own life, says Mark

---

19   For more information on Rev. Coleman and the Community Support Advisory Council (CSAC), look up www.csacsouth.org.

Twain, don't blame other people, or your circumstances, or your upbringing, or the world. "Don't go around saying the world owes you a living. The world owes you nothing. It was here first."

"Here is the test to find whether your mission on earth is finished," writes author Richard Bach. "If you're alive, it isn't." As long as you're still breathing, you have a purpose in God's great plan.

"You are not here to make a living," said President Woodrow Wilson. "You are here in order to enable the world to live more amply, with greater vision, with a finer spirit of hope and achievement."

The more you take responsibility for your past and present, the more you are able to create the future you seek.

After serving in World War I, Walt Disney moved to Kansas City to begin his artistic career. He decided he wanted to create a future in the newspaper business, drawing political caricatures or comic strips. But nobody wanted to hire him; they said he lacked creativity. He decided to start his own commercial company, which sadly had a very short life. Disney went through a number of other business failures, using up all his funds, but he kept alive the vision of creating the life he truly wanted. As we all know, in the film and entertainment industry Walt Disney succeeded beyond his wildest dreams. He did it because he remained responsible for creating the life he felt destined for.

Gilda Radner, one of the great comic geniuses of the 20th century who got her start on the television show *Saturday Night Live*, came down with ovarian cancer and died just weeks before her 43rd birthday. Spoken shortly before her death, her advice was to live with purpose. "The goal is to live a full, productive life even with all that ambiguity," she said. "No matter what happens, whether the cancer never flares up again or whether you die, the important thing is that the days that you have had you will have lived."

Humility

Acknowledging our accomplishments is life-giving and makes us feel good, yet we are taught to be humble, especially in certain religious traditions. What should one do?

First of all, you are *not* being humble when you deny your accomplishments. When a person denies his or her accomplishments in order to appear humble; it is usually a veil that covers pride under a veneer of modesty. To say that you didn't accomplish something when you actually did is not humility…it's dishonesty. Humility is when you look past your accomplishments and see that what you have become is what God made you. What you have, God gave you. Humility shows its true colors when you acknowledge that your success is rooted in God's help.

In one of his talks, psychologist John Powell spoke about humility. Here's how I recall what he said: When we look through the New Testament, Powell said, the perfect example of humility for St Jerome was what Mary, the Mother of Jesus, said when she met her cousin Elizabeth. It was a Jewish custom, when a woman was about to deliver a child, her female relatives would come to assist her. And when Elizabeth, who was about to deliver John the Baptist, sees her cousin Mary, who is herself three months pregnant, coming to help her, Elizabeth says, in effect, "Oh, Mary, you shouldn't have come." But Mary can't control her happiness. She throws herself into her cousin's arms and says, "Oh, Elizabeth, my soul magnifies the Lord; my soul makes much of the Lord. And my spirit rejoices in God, my Savior. He who is mighty has looked down upon me, His little servant girl. I had no claims on Him, and He has done such great things in me that all nations will call me blessed." Ambrose says this is the perfect expression of humility.

According to John Powell, this is the way God invites each of us to feel: God who is mighty has done great and beautiful things in me. God has made me to the divine image and likeness. God has loved me into life. God has given me great gifts. This is what humility means—to acknowledge all the good things that God has done in us and to be very grateful to God for whatever we are able to do to further God's plan. In its core, humility involves the honest admission, almost a rejoicing, in the good things that are a part of me—that are within me waiting to be expressed.

Your Special Fundamental Choice

The Fourth Fundamental Choice implies that you recognize that your life has a purpose in God's plan. You might call this a fifth, very Personal Fundamental Choice.

For example, even though Louis does some hands-on ministry to the poor, his main life's work is intellectual. "I write books that help simplify complex theological and spiritual ideas and show how these ideas can be applied in life. So each morning, I make the Personal Fundamental Choice: *To live this day to foster spiritual growth wherever I can.* I also ghostwrite books for people who want to make a needed contribution to the world but lack the time and skills. In this way, I help them make their contribution."

In contrast, Patricia is a counselor. She does not feel called to scholarly research and book writing as Louis does. Most of her work is one-on-one with individual clients who are emotionally hurting. Louis could never do that kind of work. So, each morning she makes her own Personal Fundamental Choice: *To live this day as an instrument of God's love and healing.*

If you know your life's calling well enough, you may be able to formulate your own personal fundamental choice.

On the Internet, we found a list of more than a hundred people, all from the State of Washington, who had made Personal Fundamental Choices to serve their communities and the Earth in various areas of need. Here are a few:

Shelly Ament, of Sequim, WA, is a wildlife biologist who chose to spend her years protecting wildlife through professional, educational and volunteer activities.

Laura Jane Bailey, of Seattle, made the Personal Fundamental Choice to spend at least part of each day visiting elderly, homebound and hospitalized individuals.

Celeste Brady, of Issaquah, volunteers as a dance teacher at Hazen High School bringing the rich culture of Mexico to the students.

David Corner, of Tacoma, formed The Gathering Project, a non-profit organization whose mission is to donate household items, student supplies, technology, medical supplies and equipment to countries whose people need these resources.

B. Timothy Dolby, of Tumwater, was the primary force behind a drive to establish a dental clinic in Olympia's Union Gospel Mission. The clinic is free and sees low-income patients with no insurance or means to pay for dental care.

Henry Eisenhardt, of Seattle, who loved the game of chess, decided to start a program that taught schoolchildren to play chess. His volunteer group provides the chess equipment and the instructors to teach the children. The program now reaches 1,400 students at 40 schools.

The Inspiration for Writing This Book

This book is dedicated to a friend of Louis' for over fifty years who committed his life to the poor in an inner city neighborhood of Baltimore. Each morning he made the Personal Fundamental Choice: *To live this day in my neighborhood as a witness to hope.*

Not many people know, even among his many friends, the story of how Father Tom Composto first dedicated his life *to* the St Francis Neighborhood Center and *for* the people in its neighborhood. It was in 1963. Some of Tom's fellow Jesuits at Woodstock College, near Ellicott City, Maryland, suggested Tom might like to do some ministry at the St Francis Center in a black ghetto in Baltimore. A few years before, some Jesuits from Woodstock had started the St Francis Center. So, one morning Tom drove to the Center, which was then located on Whitelock Street.

When Tom drove up to the Center that morning, an older African-American came up to Tom's car window. Tom lowered the window and said hello.

Then the older man said to Tom, "Are you one of those Jesuit fellows working at the Center?"

Tom said, he wasn't working there yet, but he was thinking about coming here to do ministry.

Then the older man said to Tom, "I hope you're not going to be like the rest of those fellows. They come here to serve the neighborhood, they stay for a few months or a year, and then they leave, and we never see them again."

Then, in words that had to have been inspired by God, Tom made his Personal Fundamental Choice and said to the man, "If I come here to serve the neighborhood, the Center will be my home. I will stay here with you people till I die."

And that's what Tom Composto did. He never went back on his word. He kept his promise for almost 50 years—till the day he died! To many in the neighborhood he brought hope. He rid the nearby streets of drug dealers. He also found ways to offer to his neighbors healthcare, dental care, remedial education, addiction counseling, bible study, music lessons and many other needed services. Besides hope, his biggest gifts to his neighborhood were his compassion and caring.

At his funeral service, a hundred crammed themselves into the Center and hundreds more stood in the yard or on the sidewalk and street. With police escort, as in a New Orleans style funeral, his coffin was carried all around the neighborhood with all the hundreds of mourners following the coffin and singing the Negro spiritual "I'll Fly Away."

When I die, hallelujah by and by, I'll fly away.
Some bright morning when this life is over, I'll fly away
To a land on God's celestial shore, I'll fly away...[20]

Another part of Tom's story is that, some time during the 1980s, his religious superiors from New York ordered him to move back to New York. Tom told his superiors that he had made a promise to the people in his neighborhood—and to God—that he would never leave them. Apparently, his superiors thought lightly of such a promise, for they issued an ultimatum to Tom. They said, in effect, "Either return to New York, or we will dismiss you from the Jesuit Order. You will no longer be a Jesuit."

Tom remained faithful to his promise to stay in his Baltimore neighborhood among his people. His superiors dismissed him from the Jesuit Order. So, Tom gave up his treasured Jesuit identity in order to stay faithful to his promise to the people of his neighborhood.

Whatever your gifts, whatever your abilities, create your personal Fundamental Choice in such a way that you use your gifts as an instrument of God's work in the world.

---

20 "I'll Fly Away," written by Albert E. Brumley in 1929, is probably the most recorded gospel music song of all times. It inspired a television series by the same name. The hymn was also sung many times by Jason on *The Waltons*.

Conclusion

Living provides a fascinating experience. The amazing reality is that we're all living together on Earth—millions of species, 30,000 different life forms, about seven-billion people, and all of us thriving each in our own ways, existing, co-existing and in co-creation mode.

The wonderful part of it is that as part of God's grand plan each of us seven-billion humans are being called upon to help make that plan a reality, and to offer our own personal contributions to it.

We ground ourselves in that grand project by making the four Fundamental Choices each day. And a special personal, fifth one, too.

Shortstop Jackie Robinson, in 1949 was the first African-American to play in major league baseball in the United States. "Life is not a spectator sport," he said. "If you're going to spend your whole life in the grandstand just watching what goes on, in my opinion you're wasting your life."

"One is not born into the world to do everything," wrote Henry David Thoreau, "but to do something."

Chapter 7

The Little Way

Although many will be called by God to do important things in helping renew the face of Earth, all of us—even those who are Earth-shakers—spend most of our days doing things that are seemingly very mundane and unimportant.

Paleontologists spend hours and days bending over in the hot sun sifting through sand in hopes of finding one ancient fossil.

Research chemists spend days and months in their laboratories watching chemical experiments hoping for some sign of success.

Housekeepers spend much time in the home dusting furniture surfaces that will only become dusty again or cleaning kitchen counters that will only get messed up again.

Customer service representatives sitting in cramped cubicles hooked to telephones answer the same old caller questions a hundred times every day.

Workers at the car wash spend all day scrubbing dirt spots off car surfaces.

Housekeeping staff in hotels make beds all day long, day after day, week after week, month after month.

Laundry workers and dry cleaners fold and press clothing and linens all day long.

Office paperwork. Filling out forms. Deleting computer spam. All of it meticulous and boring.

No matter how exalted your position or job may be, it is usually full of seemingly unimportant actions and interactions—things that must be done when you'd like to be doing something else.

We are tempted to think that these boring and very ordinary human actions and interactions are of little or no consequence in the great plans that God has for humanity and the rest of creation. Where, we might wonder, could we ever find a way to transform these habitual humdrum bits and pieces of life into something valuable to God's vast, eternal plan?

One of the easiest and best ways to transform ordinary tasks is to follow what St. Thérèse of Lisieux called her "Little Way." It is a "way" of living where *you do each little thing—no matter how boring or distasteful—with love and care.* It is a way we can all adopt, and it will certainly help in small ways to renew the face of our Earth.

"Think of small acts of kindness in the same way as compound interest—a little bit over a long time runs into great riches," wrote Nancy Hancock in *Spirit of Service.* "Send a two-sentence postcard to a friend having a tough time. Take one piece of trash out of a teenager's room. Drop a quarter in the tip jar at the cash register."[21]

Renewing Earth is like constructing a building. Those who do important things symbolize the foundations, steel beams, concrete blocks, layers of bricks and rafters of wood that give the building its predominant structure and shape. However, all the little daily acts of loving and caring symbolize the unnoticed nails, screws, bolts, plaster and glue that keep the bigger parts together. Both are essential. God's plan involves many big things, but many thousands more little things.

To all of us who feel we can do nothing big or impressive, St. Thérèse is a reminder that it is the little things done with loving care that keep God's project going forward and hold God's world together. Without millions of small acts of love and caring that people do every day, it is likely the human race would quickly fall apart.

Even those who do great things in helping carry out God's plan are expected to incorporate into their spiritual practices ways to make the monotonous, tedious and boring things of their lives useful and valuable.

St. Thérèse never founded a religious order; she never performed great works and never went on missions. Yet, she understood that what matters in life is not great deeds, but great love, and that anyone can achieve the heights of spirituality and help transform the world by doing even the smallest things well for love of God.

---

21 Nancy Hancock *Spirit of Service.* New York: HarperCollins, 2009, p. 103.

Her daily life as a nun was made up of many little things, most of them tedious and boring: weeding in the garden, peeling potatoes in the kitchen, dusting the convent stairs, sewing and mending torn clothing, cleaning the animal stalls, scrubbing sinks, sweeping the corridors, picking vegetables and preparing them, cleaning the bedpans of the sick nuns, listening to the older nuns tell the same stories over and over, and so on.

If you have ever prayed and meditated for long periods, day after day, you will know that prayer times are not always filled with consolation and ecstasies. Such blissful experiences are the rare exceptions. Mostly, hours in the chapel become routine and lead to sleepy head-nodding. It is in this context of doing a thousand little things that Thérèse discovered and practiced her Little Way.

Steps for the Little Way

Her Little Way is quite simple, but not always easy. Anyone can follow it. It applies primarily to work that may be routine and dreary. It applies to tedious conversations and interactions, wherever you may be. It applies to every conversation, no matter how unimportant. It applies to every facet and moment of your life.

Here are her "little way" steps:

- *Do each step or element of your daily work with the intention of pleasing God and helping further God's plan just a little bit more.*
- *Do each little action as an expression of your love for God, for humanity and for God's Earth.*
- *If you do it with love in your heart—no matter what it is—you can be confident that it is helping carry out what God wants of you. It is a part of God's plan and God's plan for you.*
- *If you fail or miss a chance to do something in a loving way, know that God still loves you infinitely and forgives you before you even realize it.*
- *If you err, just smile, say thanks to God for God's love and forgiveness, and go back to your daily duties as lovingly as you can.*

St. Thérèse called her spirituality "the little way of spiritual childhood." It is based upon a complete and unshakeable confidence in God's love for us. This childlike confidence means that there is no need to be afraid of God even though we stumble and fail. For God knows—and we know—that, being human, we shall inevitably not always live up to our potential. After each fall, God is ready to forgive us. God comes to meet us with grace to help us get to our feet again. God wants us to continue the work we are doing for God.

St. Thérèse does not minimize the gravity of sin, but she insists that we must not be crushed by it. We have only to repent and realize that God's love never fails. And God's love for us must be matched, within our human limitations, by our love for God and what God is doing in the world.

By following this little way of loving, it creates a ceaseless flow of love—back and forth—between Creator and creatures. Once you let yourself feel this interchange of love, it does away with the feeling that to please God you must do great and extraordinary things.

In Thérèse's own words, she discovers that her love becomes tremendously powerful because God is letting her "borrow" God's divine love to use as her own. She says to God,

Love attracts love, mine rushes forth unto Thee. It would fill up, if it could, the abyss of Love that attracts it. But alas! My act of love is not even like one drop of dew lost in the Ocean. To love Thee as Thou love me I must borrow Thy very Love. Then only can I find rest.

"Only a handful of people knew anything of Thérèse during her short life, for she entered Carmel when she was fifteen, and few knew or cared that she was dead at twenty-four. Less than thirty years after her death, however, she was canonized a saint."[22] That is miraculous speed for Rome!

The following year she was declared with St. Francis Xavier, the principal patron of all missionaries and missions, even though she had never left the confines of her Carmelite convent, such was considered the power of her prayer for missionaries. Later she was declared the secondary patron of France with St. Joan of Arc. And most recently she was made a Doctor of the Church, because of her theology of the spiritual life—her Little Way.

---

22 *Autobiography of Saint Thérèse of Lisieux: The Story of a Soul.* New York: Doubleday, 1957 trans. by John Beevers. From the Introduction. p. vii.

The Story of a Soul

What made the difference in Thérèse's popularity after her death was that her Mother Superior had told her to write about her childhood and life. Apparently, in the Carmelite convents it was customary, when a nun was growing old or likely to die, that the nun be asked to write about her life, so that other nuns may read it after her death and remember her as a member of the community. How grateful we are to that Mother Superior!

The Story of a Soul that the twenty-three year old Thérèse, dying of tuberculosis, wrote became a classic work in spirituality. Translated into thirty-eight languages, Thérèse's autobiography became perhaps the best-selling spiritual book of the 20th century.

Now, if you think about it, Thérèse's memoire was never written as a book. Over a period of months, she scribbled her thoughts and memories quickly, snatching moments of free time during the evening or while sitting in the garden. Much of it was written when she knew she was dying, suffering the pain and distress of a terminal illness. Her writings were never corrected or edited for style. Nevertheless, without the literary quality of Augustine's *Confessions*, Thérèse's hurriedly written notes became one of the most widely read spiritual books in history.

Although the world came to view Thérèse as one of the splendid roses or lilies of God, she saw herself as a "God's Little Flower," one of the tiny daises or violets in God's garden.

Shortly before she died Thérèse told her superior: "What I have written will do a lot of good. It will make the kindness of God better known." At some level, even then, she was aware that she was God's gift to the world, and that writing her book was part of her contribution to God's grand project.

Love of Creation

What is often not noticed is that Thérèse loved creation with the same purity and intensity that she loved God and her fellow humans. She recognized, as St. Paul did, that nature and all creation has the same inbuilt longing to be with God that humans have. Creation groans for its fulfillment just as we humans do:

For the creation waits with eager longing for the revealing of the children of God; for the creation was subjected to futility, not of its own will but by the will of the one who subjected it, in hope that the creation itself will be set free from its bondage to decay and will obtain the freedom of the glory of the children of God. We know that the whole creation has been groaning in labor pains until now; and not only the creation, but we ourselves, who have the first fruits of the Spirit, groan inwardly while we wait for adoption, the redemption of our bodies. (Rom 8:19-23)

When Thérèse read these words of St. Paul, she saw groaning creation as the millions of flowers in the fields, the vegetables in her garden, the birds in the trees, the rocks, the soil itself, the sun, moon and stars. She loved each of them because they were expressions of God's love given to her. She realized that to love a flower is to love God, to pick lovingly a green bean growing on the vine is to love God, to enjoy sitting in the shade of a tree is to love God's gift of nature.

In Thérèse's era (1873-1897), there were many who saw the world as evil and bad, full of temptations, and a sure road to hell. Thérèse was able to realize that God loved every creature and every human with an infinite love, as did her beloved Jesus himself.

Few ever notice that, early in the *Gospel According to John*, Jesus proclaims God's love for all that exists. When Jesus is speaking to Nicodemus, he makes this startling comment.

"For God so loved the world that he gave his only Son, so that everyone who believes in him may not perish but may have eternal life. Indeed, God did not send the Son into the world to condemn the world, but in order that the world might be saved through him." (John 3: 16-17)

When most people read those two verses, they focus on their personal salvation and having "eternal life." But instead, focus on the word "world." In the Greek text, the word Jesus uses for "world" is "the cosmos," namely all of creation—everything that exists. That first verse tells us *how intensely God loved all of creation. God loved it as much as he loved his own Son.* That's very passionate love, and Jesus is saying that God has that kind of passionate love for all that exists—creation.

The second sentence reminds us that God sent the Son, not to condemn what God had created, but to save it, that is, to bring all of creation—the world—to its destined fulfillment. God does not condemn. God's love turns everything into gift.

This is what Thérèse knew. This was the secret behind her little way. God's love gave life to every flower and weed, so God could be loved and adored through every little flower and weed. God could be loved peeling potatoes—God was in the potato peels themselves. God could be loved while dusting the stairs—God was giving existence to the dust itself. God's presence could be found everywhere. God could be loved in and through everything—absolutely everything. Thérèse realized she was living surrounded by God in everything she could see or hear or smell or touch.

One of the most famous Jesuits of the 20th century was Pierre Teilhard de Chardin. He was born in France less than ten years after St. Thérèse. He grew up surrounded by a spirituality that was very either/or. It said essentially, "Love God and hate the world. You can't love both." Teilhard refused to hate the world, because, like Thérèse, he knew that God loved it intensely. So, Teilhard began to teach that we can love both God and the world passionately. We can love God in loving and protecting the natural world. Teilhard knew that God loved creation passionately, so why shouldn't we?

Both Thérèse and Teilhard are revealing the same "little way" to us

Another French nun, Mother Thérèse Couderc, founder of the Religious of the Cenacle, had a different experience of God's love for every person and every thing. Whenever we buy a product, we notice that the name of the maker is printed on the label, or the labels sewn into clothing identify the brand name. One day, when Mother Thérèse was at prayer, she began to notice that each thing she looked at had God's brand name stamped on it. Her prayer bench had God's label on it. Her bed had God's label on it. When she walked outdoors, every tree and flower had God's brand name stamped on it. When she saw a Sister passing by, God's label was on that Sister. No matter where she looked, she saw God's personal label on each little thing. God was telling her that God and the products of God's love were everywhere, absolutely everywhere.

We may not have the mystical experience of seeing God's label on everything around us, but we know the truth of her experience. It tells each of us that, as God's gifts to the world, God is working through all the elements and forces of the universe to bring about the grand divine project. And whatever we desire to contribute to the success of that grand project, God and the universe is supporting us.

There are three most important things we seek to learn from prayer.

- *How to find God in all things*
- *How to love what God loves*
- *How to love the way God loves.*

Chapter 8

For God's Greater Glory

Expanding Your Generosity

Even while you are using St. Thérèse's way of loving God through all the little things you do, your challenge now is to begin creating things that expand your generosity. Don't set limits on what you can or cannot do for God. Good ideas are a dime a dozen, but people who put them into action are priceless. They are the ones who help renew the face of the Earth. That's why you are so valuable to God.

As Saint Thérèse would say to you:

- *May you trust that you are exactly where you are meant to be.*
- *May you not forget the infinite possibilities that are born of faith.*
- *May you use those gifts that you have received,*
- *And pass on the love that has been shown to you.*

Some Generous People

Tommy Alday, born on a Georgia farm, developed there a work ethic of resourcefulness and generosity. He came to Florida and, using his resourcefulness and generosity, became wealthy as founder of a real estate title company. Later in life, one of his favorite acts of generosity was to buy a box full of Starbucks $10 gift cards and hand them out to people at the door. As one of his colleagues remarked, "If Tommy saw somebody walk up to a Starbucks and they didn't have a smile on their face, he would stop them, give them a Starbucks gift card and say, 'Just smile.'"

From his farm in Florida, he gave his prized cattle to high schools so the Future Farmers of America (FFA) could raise money for scholarships. "He never asked for anything in return," said his daughter Michelle. "He just wanted to go to the fair to see those kids showing their cows."

Some people faced eviction. Others may never have had a home. Maybe a family's plight had appeared in a newspaper story, or Tommy Alday heard about a terminally ill child. "All got a messenger's knock on the door and an envelope containing cash. They didn't know who sent it, and the messenger would never say." Tommy's giving was always anonymous.[23]

Edna Ligon spent 21 years of her working life in the dietary department at St. Joseph Hospital in Tampa. Now in retirement, she's back in the kitchen—as a volunteer at New Salem Baptist Church in Tampa. A member there since 1957, she does the church's grocery shopping and manages sixteen volunteers who prepare weekly Sunday meals for the poor and special fare for weddings and funerals. "I have bad knees and can't sit still too long," she said. "Keeping busy helps me stay well, helps me get going."[24]

Ignatius Loyola, founder of the Jesuits, had a motto, AMDG, which members of his group often write at the top of their correspondence. AMDG stands for *Ad Majoram Dei Gloriam*, which is Latin for "For the Greater Glory of God."

Notice, the motto does not say, "For the Glory of God" and not even "For the Great Glory of God" but "For the *Greater* Glory of God." This means you can always do more. You can always do something *greater* for the glory of God. There are always ways to expand your creativity and generosity.

Ignatius knew that God was doing something special in the world and with the world. He sensed that God had a great project going, great plans for creation. Ignatius also knew that we humans were meant to cooperate in God's grand project—to renew the face of the Earth. And it was not enough for any of his men to sit on their laurels, no matter

23 Andrew Meacham, "Epilogue: Tommy Alday," *St. Petersburg Times*, December 5, 2010, 4B.

24 Dawn Morgan Elliott, "You Only Get What You Give," TampaDoGooder. Blogspot.com.

how much good each one had already done. There was always more to be done.

Ignatius has his men pray for generosity in doing God's work:

> Lord, teach me to be generous.
> Teach me to serve you as you deserve;
> to give and not to count the cost....
> to labor and not to ask for reward,
> save that of knowing that I do your will.

For Ignatius, as long as you were still breathing you had a purpose, a divine purpose. There was a saying that Jesuits died with their boots on. That meant, till the last moment of life, a Jesuit was out doing God's work. Jesuits never "retired."

Jesus once said, "Be you perfect as your heavenly Father is perfect." That word "perfect" has proved to be a confusing English translation of a beautiful Aramaic concept. As we know, when Jesus spoke to the crowds or to his disciples, he used the ancient Aramaic language, the common language in which Jews spoke to one another. The most common meaning of the Aramaic word Jesus used (which we translate as "perfect") was "all-embracing." So, Jesus was telling us that his heavenly Father holds close and embraces everyone and everything with love. God is all-embracing. Perhaps, Jesus was trying to say to us, "Learn to love the way my heavenly Father loves, in an all-embracing way." Hold everyone and everything close to your heart.

Until we all learn to love creation and each other, enemies included, in this all-embracing way, God cannot renew the face of the Earth. God's grand project cannot be done without us. That is why we are God's gift to the world. This is why Ignatius wanted to teach each of his companions how to love each other and those they served in this all-embracing way, the way God loves and serves.

By learning to love in this all-embracing way, we are helping to change the face of the Earth. And the reason we do it is AMDG—For the Greater Glory of God. And the best way to give greater glory to God is through loving each other the way God loves us.

Two Principles of Loving

According to St. Ignatius, in the way God loves us we can observe two fundamental principle of loving. The first:

Love manifests itself more by deeds than words.

Loving words are always welcomed, of course. No one can deny that. However, in most cases, action is the truest manifestation of love. Your loving action is the guarantee that your loving words are sincere. Or as Jane Addams, founder of Hull House for the poor, put it, "Action is indeed the sole medium of expression for ethics." And unselfish action is usually the most loving ethical action.

Action is the heart and soul of the commitment people make who volunteer to serve in AmeriCorps. When volunteers take the AmeriCorps Pledge, they say: "I will get things done for America—to make our people safer, smarter and healthier." Many volunteers have discovered that the true meaning of life is to plant trees, under whose shade they do not expect to sit. The fact is that most of the people in future generations who will enjoy the shade of those trees—and other things that our generation has started—will have no idea who planted them.

President Ronald Reagan put another perspective on loving action. "No matter how big and powerful government gets, and the many services it provides, it can never take the place of volunteers."

Philosopher William James said, "The great use of your life is to spend it for something that outlasts it."

"Volunteers," said Erma Bombeck, the good-natured Jewish lady who wrote many books of wisdom sprinkled with much humor, "are the only human beings on the face of the Earth who reflect this nation's compassion, unselfish caring, patience, and just plain love for one another."

All Over the World

Many volunteers do their work all over the world in hundreds of countries. Peace Corps members, numbering almost nine thousand, range in age from 18 (minimum age) to 86. They serve in 77 countries, as teachers, engineers, nurses, physicians, dentists, farmers, beauticians, carpenters, plumbers, technicians, computer operators, foreign language teachers, lawyers, financial advisors, well builders, home builders, counselors, and a host of other community-building functions practical and interpersonal. The usual Peace Corps stint is for 27 months, at pay that doesn't exceed $300 a month. Members give of their time and talents willingly and generously.

Recently, we have noticed the creative generosity of certain celebrities who do more than contribute money or donate an evening of their time to mingle with potential donors at a fundraiser for charity. Today, film stars are spending time in the field all over the developing world and, at home, meeting with policymakers.

Angelina Jolie has been the United Nations' advocate for refugees since 2001, having visited more than twenty countries. With partner Brad Pitt she started a foundation to fight rural poverty.

Matt Damon, inspired by his role in the film *Running the Sahara* that told the story of the water shortage in North Africa has started a foundation called H_2O Africa providing microloans to communities to build wells and sanitation processes.

Rock star Bono created a number of fund raising programs to combat global poverty, and had meetings with international leaders to advocate for debt forgiveness for poor countries.

Sean Penn has been part of a group working on site with rebuilding temporary housing for 50,000 refugees in Haiti after the earthquake there as well as providing medical care for many more.

Alicia Keys is cofounder of Keep a Child Alive that provides medicine for HIV and support for AIDS orphans in Africa.

Since 2006, George Clooney has been involved in the peaceful achievement of independence for the people of South Sudan in Africa.

These are just a few of the many celebrities who have found time to become deeply personally involved in projects that are much bigger than their own Hollywood careers.

You may not have the financial or public resources that these stars have, but you can put your heart and creativity into projects that make a difference in your community. Volunteer to deliver Meals on Wheels for a few hours a week. Visit lonely people in a nursing home, read to them, chat a while or just smile and hold their hand. Give someone something they may need—a coat, a sweater, a small loan. On the sidewalk, stop for a moment to say something friendly and encouraging to the old man with the cane who is trying to keep moving and stay healthy. Put some money in the Poor Box at your church. Donate used books or magazines to places that can use them, like jails, nursing homes, etc. Give somebody who doesn't have a car a ride to church or to a doctor's appointment. Take a casserole to a lonely widower or to anyone too depressed to cook for themselves. Plant a flower in your yard. Give compliments freely and often.

It's not necessary to have a grand and exalted purpose for your life. As advice columnist Carolyn Hax observed: "I'd say that society benefits when there's variety in what people see as their life purpose. People with small ambitions, quiet lives, or just a knack for fun bring needed balance to people with grand ambitions. Someone needs to tend the gardens and bake cookies with the kids…What matters, I think, is that you bring more to the world than you take away. That's a good life. The details are up to you."[25]

Sometimes we let ourselves think that our small acts of kindness and generosity seem to make no difference. But no matter how unproductive, hidden, pointless or insignificant that small act of caring may seem to you, it is welcomed by God. Every act of generous self-giving, no matter how small, is never lost for it connects us instantly with the great work God is doing. It allows God's love to manifest itself in some new way. It also allows something of the potential inside you to reveal itself, something you may not have been aware of before. In her book *The Wisdom Jesus*, Cynthia Bourgeault calls this inner revelation a kind of "sacred alchemy," where what seems to be worthless is turned into something of great value. What happens in this process is that our self-giving is transformed into God's self-giving. She writes:

"As we practice in daily life, in our acts of compassion, kindness and self-emptying, both at the level of our doing and even more at the level of our being, something is catalyzed out of that self-emptying which is pure divine substance mirrored in our own true face. Subtle qualities of divine

25 Carolyn Hax, "Advice: Tell Me About It," *The Washington Post*. tellme@washpost.com.

love essential to the well being of this planet are released through our actions and flow out into the world as miracle, healing and hope."[26]

The act of self-giving brings new awareness into being. Whenever you create something new, you also reveal something new about yourself. When you study God's creation, you begin to understand what God is like in new and different ways. According to the Judeo-Christian tradition, in the beginning God spoke the creative Word and said, "Let there be light." And the universe exploded into existence. Creation was God, in an extravagant self-emptying, self-giving act of loving generosity. In that moment, God was revealing God's very Self to us, though we would not realize it until almost 14 billion years later.

Self-giving is also at the same time self-communicating. Creation was God's form of self-communicating. Whenever you make a difference in the world, you are communicating yourself to the world, but also communicating something new about yourself to yourself.

In every positive action or gesture you make, you are also communicating God's love to the world—and to yourself.

The Divine Alchemy

Just as God is transforming every smallest, most insignificant positive gesture into the work of bringing the grand divine project toward its completion, so God is using this same sacred alchemy to transform even the basest deeds, even those that seem utterly unredeemable or without any hope of saving grace. Cynthia Bourgeault reports the work of an unknown poet living in a Nazi death camp during World War II. It was a prayer left behind near the body of a dead child:

> *O Lord, remember not only the men and women of good will,*
> *But also those of ill will.*
> *But do not remember all the suffering they inflicted on us.*
> *Remember the fruits we have bought, thanks to this suffering—*
> *Our comradeship, our loyalty,*
> *Our humility, our courage,*
> *Our generosity, the greatness of heart*

---

26 Cynthia Bourgeault, *The Wisdom Jesus.* Boston: Shambala, 2008, p. 73.

Which has grown out of all this.
And when they come to judgment,
Let all the fruits which we have borne
Be their forgiveness.

Here in this prayer, writes Bourgeault, "but particularly in its completely surprising final word, the divine alchemy is supremely at work, showing its power to turn even the deepest hardness of cruelty and atrocity into something new and soft and flowing. *And the template for that alchemy is imprinted in our soul.*"[27]

"I have found the paradox that if I love until it hurts," said Mother Teresa, "then there is no hurt, but only more love."

The Second Principle of Loving

The second basic principle in the way God loves us is:

Love consists in a mutual communication and sharing between two persons.

Even though the first principle of loving asserts that love is shown in actions more than words, the second principle does not want us to forget about using words. Talking to each other is an essential first step in loving. Once people are communicating and mutually respecting each other, they begin to share with each other what they have. They begin to give each other gifts. Ignatius mentions three areas for mutual sharing and mutual gift-giving: *knowledge, honor* and *riches.* These are the things we are to share with others.

Sandra Day O'Connor, Justice of the Supreme Court, had the same insight about loving that Ignatius had when she said, "If we focus our energies on sharing ideas, finding solutions and using what is right with America to remedy what is wrong with it, we can make a difference. Our nation needs bridges, and bridges are built by those who look to the future and dedicate themselves to helping others."

Helen Keller reinforced much the same thought. "Until the great

---

27 Bourgeault, p. 73-4. Italics added.

mass of the people shall be filled with the sense of responsibility for each other's welfare, social justice can never be attained."

"If everyone howled at every injustice, every act of barbarism, every act of unkindness," wrote novelist Nelson DeMille, "then we would be taking the first step towards a real humanity."

This "real humanity" that DeMille speaks of gives us a sense of God's project. Jesus didn't use the expression "God's Project." He called it "The Kingdom of God" and "The Kingdom of Heaven." Many Christians assume that the Kingdom of Heaven is where you go after you die—provided you have been good. But that is not the way Jesus saw it. In fact, Jesus himself specifically contradicts this interpretation. He said, "The Kingdom of Heaven is *within you*" and "The Kingdom of Heaven is *at hand*." If it is within you, that means it's *here*. If it is at hand, that means it's *now*. It's already in process, even though we do not have the eyes to see it. Bourgeault writes, "It [the Kingdom of Heaven] is not later, but *lighter*—some more subtle quality of dimension of experience accessible to you right in the moment. You don't die into it; you awaken into it."[28] It's imprinted in our soul waiting to be awakened.

Each of us has the capacity, if we choose, to shift into this new and different way of perceiving. Some have called this "seeing with the eyes of the heart," for they view the "heart" primarily as an organ of spiritual perception. We come into this life equipped with that special ability "to see with the eyes of the heart." That ability is waiting inside us, waiting to be awakened. If you choose to awaken into it, you will learn that you can guide your life by it, understand everything through it, and ultimately discover your deepest self and purpose within it. That is the magical transformation waiting to be awakened in each of us.

In 2008, J. K. Rowling, author of the famous Harry Potter fantasy books about students at Hogworts, a fictional school of magic, spoke the following words to the students at the Harvard University commencement ceremonies. "We do not need magic to transform the world. We carry all the power we need inside ourselves already. We have the power to imagine better."

I end my book with some affirmations:

---

28 Bourgeault, p. 30.

Promise me you'll always remember:
You're braver than you believe,
and stronger than you seem,
and smarter than you think.
But the most important thing is,
Even if we're apart,
I'll always be with you.

Those affirmations don't come from me, but from Christopher Robin speaking to Pooh. But they are the same affirmations we all need to keep saying to each other every day, if we are to live out our destiny as God's gifts to the world.

SELECT BIBLIOGRAPHY

Arjuna Ardagh, *The Translucent Revolution: How People Just Like You are WAKING UP and CHANGING the World*. Novato, CA: New World Library, 2005.

"It's a rather extraordinary, even historical time we live in, and not just for the perils but the promise. The perils I'm sure you've heard plenty of. This is a book about the promise..." Those are the words of a contemporary philosopher, Ken Wilbur, in a Foreword he wrote for Ardagh's book. It is a mammoth book of over 500 pages revealing, as it's subtitle announces, how ordinary people are waking up and changing their world.

Cynthia Bourgeault, *The Wisdom Jesus*. Boston: Shambala, 2008. She presents Jesus as a wisdom teacher, who shows us the way to live as God's gift to the world.

Robert Fritz, *The Path of Least Resistance: Learning to Become the Creative Force in Your Own Life*. New York: Random House, 1984. For the power of choice, especially fundamental choices.

Victor Goertzel and Mildred G. Goertzel, *Cradles of Eminence*. Boston: Little, Brown, 1962. They researched the childhood stories of over 400 famous twentieth-century men and women and the parents who gave birth to them.

Yitta Halberstam and Judith Leventhal, *Small Miracles: Extraordinary Coincidences from Everyday Life*. Holbrook, MA: Adams Media Corporation, 1997. And *Small Miracles II: Heartwarming Gifts of Extraordinary Coincidences*. 1998. Both books are full of inspiring stories of miraculous coincidences, each one hinting that God is quietly working in us and among us.

Nancy Hancock, *Spirit of Service: Your Daily Stimulus for Making a Difference*. San Francisco: HarperOne, 2009. If you are already eager and looking for ways to make a difference in your community, this book puts you in touch with over 500 organizations just as eagerly waiting for you.

Paul Hawken, *Blessed Unrest: How the Largest Movement in the World Came into Being and Why No One Saw It Coming*. New York: Viking, 2007. Hawken describes "the growth of a worldwide movement that is determined to heal the wounds of the earth with the force of passion, dedication and collective intelligence and wisdom." This is not the movement of a single group, but of at least two million separate groups, large and small, all over the planet committed to healing the wounds in their own communities and nations. Hawken characterizes this movement a "new type of charity" or love of neighbor and Earth, that includes but stretches beyond the missions of specifically religious groups.

Sue Monk Kidd & Ann Kidd Taylor. *Traveling with Pomegranates: A Mother-Daughter Story*. New York: Viking, 2009. The inspiring story of two women who share the process of their struggle to discern their true callings in life.

Brad Meltzer, *Heroes for My Son*. New York: HarperCollins, 2010. Short summaries of the lives of scores of heroes for young people.

Pierre Teilhard de Chardin, *The Divine Milieu*. New York: Harper, 1960. *The Phenomenon of Man*, 1959. Teilhard was the first to show that there was an inbuilt direction to evolution—from ever-increasing complexity to ever higher levels of consciousness. For a more contemporary explanation of Teilhard's spirituality, you might want to look at two of my books from Paulist Press, *The Divine Milieu Explained*, 2008, and *The New Spiritual Exercises in the Spirit of Teilhard de Chardin*, 2011.

ACKNOWLEDGEMENTS

I am extremely grateful to all of the people whom I quote in these pages, many of whose inspirational words I found on various websites. The Internet spewed out hundreds of lists of famous people's comments appropriate to themes in this book, a task that would have taken me years to do without today's computer search engines. In fact, for many of these people I quoted, I probably would never have thought to check their writings. The hundreds of quotations in this book give the text a special breadth, depth and vitality.

In the many magazines that I typically peruse during lunch, I also found inspiring stories of people worldwide who were making a positive difference. The most frequent of these familiar resources I used include *The New Yorker* magazine, *Time* magazine, *Newsweek*, *Parade* magazine, *AARP Bulletin* and *AARP Magazine*, and most especially my local newspapers *The Tampa Bay Times* and *The Tampa Tribune*. In these newspapers' obituaries I found many unique stories of unknown people making a difference.

Arjuna Ardagh's book, *The Translucent Revolution: How People Just Like You Are WAKING UP and CHANGING the World,* and Paul Hawken's *Blessed Unrest: How the Largest Movement in the World Came into Being and Why No One Saw It Coming,* made me aware that millions of individuals and groups were already working as God's gifts to the world, though most of them might not describe themselves that way.

Nancy Hancock for her *Spirit of Service: Your Daily Stimulus for Making a Difference.*

For a number of story examples, I am indebted to novelist Brad Meltzer who created the wonderfully inspiring book *Heroes for My Son.*

For inspiring the chapter on coincidences, I thank Yitta Halberstam and Judith Leventhal in their two books, *Little Miracles* and *Little*

Miracles II, especially for their insights about "coincidences" that just might be miracles.

I thank Susan Jeffers for her insights on fear and overcoming it, Muriel James for her insights on passion for service in her many, many books, and Victor and Mildred Goertzel for their study of the childhoods of over 400 famous twentieth-century men and women.

I am deeply grateful to Sue Monk Kidd, author of *The Secret Life of Bees*, and her daughter, Ann Kidd Taylor, for the autobiographical sharing of their own discovery of how they learned to be God's gift to the world. Their story is told in their co-authored book *Traveling with Pomegranates: A Mother-Daughter Story*.

My deepest inspiration for this work is the French Jesuit priest Pierre Teilhard de Chardin. Inspired by St. Paul, Teilhard realized that God has a great plan for creation and each of us has a part to play in fulfilling that great plan.

I also received encouragement from John Grim and Mary Ellen Tucker of the American Teilhard Association and Arthur Fabel, editor of *Teilhard Perspective*.

My dearest wife and partner, Patricia H. Berne, suggested the title and structure for the book, gave me many examples for the text from her own experience and from that of her children and grandchildren as well as the many friends, associates and contacts that have shared their life stories and wisdom with her. She led me to many more stories, and strongly encouraged me at every step of the way, as she agreed to read and comment on every paragraph I wrote. She caught misleading inferences in some of my sentences that she knew I did not want to convey and in many cases showed me how to say what I really wanted to.

Father Tom Composto, to whom I dedicated this book, was the living inspiration of this task for me. For he embodied someone who recognized his life as a gift from God to the world and used that gift in hundreds of ways throughout his life at the St. Francis Neighborhood Center in Baltimore. He called me a "dearest friend," a privilege I proudly enjoyed for almost fifty years.

I must mention many others who, without knowing it, gave me inspiration or example or an encouraging word. Among these I include (in more or less alphabetical order): Deacon John and Julie Alvarez, Sheryle and Jeff Baker, Barbara Barski-Carrow, Cynthia Bourgeault, Kathleen Boyle, Sister Cathy Cahill, Maureen O'Connor, Carol Mitchell and the staff at the Franciscan Center in Tampa, Sandy Cahill, Tim Casey, Julie Cate, Clare Crawford-Mason and Bob Mason, Mary and Peter Esseff, Sister Rosemary Esseff, Frank Frost, Eleanor King, Deacon Greg Kovaleski, Martin and Catherine McHugh, Mary McDonnell, Mary McNamara, Jacqueline Magness and Elizabeth Roslewicz, Rev. Austin Mullen, Flo and Leo Murphy, Robin Mustain, Ruth Nelson, Sister Sadie Nesser, Blake Pace, Juliana Painter, Rev. Leonard Piotrowski, Rev. Robert Powell, Judy Burt Walker, Rita Harper, Ed Daly and others on the staff at St. Joan of Arc Church in Orleans, MA, Shayamala Raman, Rev. Charles Topper, Mary Alice and Tony Wolf.

I also want to mention the inspiration I continue to receive from the staff at St Paul Church in Tampa and especially from the St. Vincent de Paul team there who in their care for the poor are God's very special gift to the world. I know there are many others whose names I have forgotten to mention; to those also I am deeply grateful.

Too numerous to mention are all my fellow musicians and singers who, over many decades, have freely given thousands of performance hours to bring to others expressions of God's gifts of beauty, harmony and joy in music.

Louis Savary
January, 2013,